UNFORGETTABLE

Places to see
before you die

———

UNFORGETTABLE

Places to see
before you die

———

Steve Davey

BOOKS

CONTENTS

Angkor Wat · Cambodia
12

St Petersburg · Russia
18

Havana · Cuba
24

Wat Phra Kaeo · Bangkok, Thailand
30

Grand Canyon · Arizona, USA
36

Taj Mahal · Agra, India
42

Eilean Donan Castle · Scotland
48

The Alhambra · Granada, Spain
54

Aitutaki · Cook Islands
60

Pyramid of Kukulcán · Mexico
66

Venice · Italy
72

Dead Vlei · Namibia
78

Iguassu Falls · Brazil and Argentina
84

Petra · Jordan
90

College Fjord · Alaska, USA
96

Karnak Temple · Luxor, Egypt
102

Rio de Janeiro · Brazil
108

Taman Negara Rainforest · Malaysia
114

Jaisalmer Fort · India
120

Galapagos Islands · Ecuador
126

Manhattan Island · New York, USA
132

Lake Titicaca · Bolivia and Peru
138

Monet's Garden · Giverny, France
144

Ngorongoro Crater · Tanzania
150

Santorini · Greece
156

The Amphitheatre ·
Drakensberg, South Africa 162

Zanzibar · Tanzania
168

Makalu · Himalayas, Nepal
174

Lalibela · Ethiopia
180

Machu Picchu · Peru
186

Uluru · Australia
192

The Ghats · Varanasi, India
198

Heron Island ·
Great Barrier Reef, Australia 204

Lhasa · Tibet
210

Yangshuo · Guilin, China
216

Dubrovnik · Croatia
222

Ephesus · Turkey
228

The Bund · Shanghai, China
234

Samarkand · Uzbekistan
240

Killary Harbour · Ireland
246

INTRODUCTION

What is an unforgettable place? A place you will remember for the rest of your life, certainly, but to me an unforgettable place is more than that. It is the sort of place that is so special that as soon as you discover it exists you just know you have to go there. While you might remember many things about daily life from time spent in India, for example, it will have been the desire to gaze upon the timeless beauty of the Taj Mahal that prompted you to make the journey. This book contains my own selection of 40 unforgettable places.

Certain places around the world, such as the Taj Mahal, Uluru (Ayers Rock), the Grand Canyon, Manhattan and Machu Picchu, have entered our collective consciousness. All of these crop up on most people's lists of places they would love to see, and not to include them just because they are so popular would have been silly. I hope their appearance here will act as a reminder that these places really should be seen at least once in a lifetime.

I have also tried to highlight some places that are less well known and that you may never have thought of visiting. Hopefully, featuring them here will prompt you to put them firmly on your 'to do' list. The mystical city of Samarkand, the majestic hidden stone churches of Lalibela, and even the warren that is the town of Zanzibar are all places that deserve to be more widely appreciated. (The map on pages 252–3 shows the locations of all the places featured.)

I have also included what I consider to be the best of a number of 'generic' places. How many of us have said that we would love to see 'the

rainforest' or a truly phenomenal waterfall? Well, this book looks at places that I consider to be the very best of their kind: the Sossusvlei National Park is in arguably the most amazing desert in the world, Taman Negara is the oldest rainforest in the world, the Iguassu Falls has to be the best waterfall in the world, and the Ngorongoro Crater is the single most spectacular place to view wildlife in Africa.

Many of the places I have chosen are exceptional in any terms. But will you agree with my choice? I honestly doubt it. By its very nature this book is judgemental and invites disagreement. Several people have asked why Paris, for example, is not in the book, but if you had to include just one romantic European city in this list then, for me, a wintry Venice beats Paris hands down any day of the week. Everyone will have their own favourite places; their own 'unforgettables'. But these are mine – a selection based on many years of travelling.

Previous spread: Palazzo Ducale from the top of the campanile
Opposite: View from the glaciers at the foot of Makalu

I have tried to give this book immediacy. Thousands of pictures are available of many of the locations in this book, but instead of using existing, often out-of-date, images, or views that cannot be seen by the average traveller, my co-photographer, Marc Schlossman, and I decided to photograph them afresh. So we captured most of the images you see here in a period of just nine months, spending only a few days in each location. We therefore saw these places in the same way that you might see them. This is not a book of unattainable sights – if you spend three or four days in the Galapagos, or Rio, or even Venice or the Ngorongoro Crater, this is what you can expect to see. Sometimes the skies have a few more clouds than they do on postcards, but remember that we criss-crossed the world taking these pictures on a frenetic schedule. I have tried to keep some of that excitement and enthusiasm in this book.

I also wanted to provide a sense of place. Wherever practical, I have avoided sweeping generalizations and focused on one, sometimes quite specific, location. The sort of view, for example, that you could lead someone to, blindfolded, then reveal to them the world in its splendour. For New York City, this has to be Manhattan Island. For the 2000-km-long Great Barrier Reef, it has to be Heron Island – one of the few coral cays that lies directly on the reef that you can actually stay on.

Although armchair travellers will love this book, I hope it will inspire people to hit the road themselves. At a time when there is concern about terrorism, disease and all manner of political instability I have constantly had my sanity questioned for going to so many places around the world. However, in all of my flights and solo wanderings around places noted for their bad reputations, not once have I been robbed or threatened, had a bag lost by an airline or had any particularly close shaves – except literally, by a barber in the old town of Godaulia in Varanasi. I have walked on my own down Copacabana Beach at sunrise with a brace of cameras, hiked alone through rainforest, visited a Middle East virtually deserted by western tourists at the height of a war, and received nothing but courtesy and unceasing hospitality. Sure, bad things do happen when you travel, but they happen far, far less than you might expect. And, anyway, on the road you should have insurance to cover most mishaps.

Travelling brings memories, and lots of them. There will be the big, 'blockbuster' memories – the kind that friends and family will clamour to share through your photographs and postcards: sunrise at Angkor Wat, sunset at Uluru, that first view of Piazza San Marco as you arrive in Venice by boat from the airport. These are experiences you will remember, quite literally, till you die. But your search for them will also bring you smaller, personal memories that can't be replicated: joining Bedouin for a barbecue in the mountains around Petra, haggling for spices in an Uzbekistan bazaar, picnicking with an extended Tibetan family after a festival in the stunning city of Lhasa. These experiences cannot be bought. You won't get them on a commuter train or in a supermarket. The addictive quest for sights, smells, feelings and experiences will make you feel truly alive. I hope that this book inspires you to travel to at least some of these unforgettable places, and to create some indelible memories of your own.

Steve Davey, 2004

Opposite: *Machu Picchu with Huayna Picchu in the background*

1

ANGKOR WAT

Cambodia

Although the trees that surround Angkor have been tamed,
it is still possible to imagine how this ancient city was 'lost'
to the outside world for centuries until the French explorer
Henri Mahout discovered it smothered in the jungle in 1860.

Angkor was the capital of the Khmer civilization, which spanned some 500 years, until it was sacked by Thai invaders in 1431. It reached its zenith in the 12th century, first with the building of the temple that came to be known as Angkor Wat and later with the construction of Angkor Thom, a royal city-within-a-city.

The temple was built by King Suryavarman II as a representation of Mount Meru, the mythical holy centre of Hinduism. Surrounded by a large moat bridged by a stone causeway, it is a west-facing rectangular stone structure comprising

three levels. The uppermost level, formerly open only to priests and the king, is topped with four corner towers and a central sanctuary 65 metres from the ground. Originally devoted to the Hindu god Shiva, the temple later became a Wat, or Buddhist monastery, and is now accepted as a spiritual monument by the predominantly

Above: *Angkor Wat reflected in the waters*
of the north pool at sunrise
Opposite: *Novice monks on the terrace*
of the first level of Angkor Wat

Buddhist Cambodians. Images of the Buddha can be found among its vaulted galleries.

Even after more than 800 years of plundering and erosion the carvings of Angkor Wat remain exquisite and the wealth of detail is bewildering. Galleries of bas-reliefs – the longest in the world – depict scenes from the Hindu religious epic, the Mahabharata, battle scenes from Khmer history and warnings about the tortures of hell.

The temple is best seen in the golden light of early morning when the rays of the sun pick out the apsaras (celestial nymphs) carved into its walls, seeming to breathe life into them. Amid the quiet beauty, it is hard to imagine that this place was one of the final refuges of the notorious Khmer Rouge communist movement – until you notice scars from the impact of bullets on the stone of the building.

Direct flights from Bangkok in Thailand have made the temples of Angkor more accessible, and they are now visited by more tourists than ever. Most tend to gather at the north pool to photograph the reflections of the rising sun, but those seeking peace and tranquillity should head straight to the principal sanctuary of Angkor Wat. This is reached by one of four flights of steep and worn stairs, signifying just how difficult and arduous is the path to heaven. It was once the exclusive preserve of Hindu priests, but now you too can have it to yourself – providing you get there early enough.

The top level of Angkor Wat seems to have been designed for the sunrise. Golden fingers slide through the unique, stone-pillared windows and illuminate details that quickly recede in the brilliant light of the day, and some of the most beautiful apsaras – which can be found in the central

Opposite: *Looking out from the third level to the second level and surrounding trees*

Above: *Monks climbing down steps from the third level of Angkor Wat*

Right: *Bas-relief of a marching army*

sanctuary – are uncovered by the rising sun, only to be hidden in shadow again just 20 minutes later.

It can sometimes be half an hour before the first few explorers from the sunrise party reach here. Most don't bother; they go back to their hotels for breakfast, and return here later in the day, when the sun is intense and energy-sapping, and the atmosphere far from spiritual.

Other parts of the Angkor complex not to be missed are the Bayon and Ta Prohm. Built later than Angkor Wat, the Bayon is a small temple covered with giant, impassive stone faces reminiscent of

Lord Buddha, and perhaps marking the transition from Hinduism to Buddhism in the Khmer civilization. Ta Prohm is a largely ruined temple complex, with roots of banyan and kapok trees growing out of the stonework — and sometimes so much a part of it that neither would survive any attempt at separation.

Above: Apsaras carved into the principal sanctuary of Angkor Wat

Opposite: Sun shining through the pillared windows of the cloisters on the third level of Angkor Wat

Siem Reap, the nearest town to Angkor (10 km away), can be reached by plane from Bangkok, Thailand (Bangkok Air has several flights a day in both directions) or from the Cambodian capital, Phnom Penh. Alternatively, you can get there by boat across Tonle Sap. This lake trip takes most of the day but is an interesting journey. A wide range of accommodation is available in Siem Reap, from inexpensive guest houses to the exclusive Amansara Resort. Tickets for the ruins can be bought for one, three or seven days. Three days is a good amount of time – it will cost £48 (US$62) and you will need a passport photograph. The site is very spread out, but the better hotels can organize a guide with a car, or you can hire a bicycle, motorbike or motorbike-taxi from many places in town.

Angkor Wat · Cambodia

2

ST PETERSBURG
Russia

If the mention of a place can bring to mind a season, then St Petersburg conjures up winter – deepest winter. Snow-covered statues, breath rising in clouds and the Winter Palace seen through mist across the frozen River Neva.

Winter is not an easy time to visit Russia – the biting cold might restrict your sightseeing – but it is the time of year that defines both the city and the Russian people. It is also the season when the tsars used to visit St Petersburg. The Winter Palace was built to house and amuse the Russian royal family during the long dark winter months. From inside you can gaze out upon the same frosty scenes that Catherine the Great once saw, the views distorted by a covering of ice on the windows.

St Petersburg was founded by Peter the Great in 1703, and the Winter Palace was completed in 1762. The founding of a European-style city on the western border of the country, and the moving of the capital from 'Asiatic' Moscow in the east, marked a Europeanization of Russia. The House of Romanov became one of the great ruling dynasties of Europe, rivalling even the Bourbons and the Habsburgs. The Winter Palace is probably their greatest creation.

St Petersburg itself has been at the centre of European history for 300 years. Revolution was fermented in the city, and the tsars were overthrown when the Bolsheviks stormed the Winter Palace in 1917, ushering in more than

70 years of Communism for Russia. St Petersburg was renamed Leningrad by the new regime and became one of the bulwarks that held up the spread of Nazism during the Second World War; a heroic defence that saw the city all but destroyed. Reverting to the old name of St Petersburg following the fall of Communism was a gesture that marked the demise of the old Soviet Union and the re-emergence of Russia.

Throughout all this history, the Winter Palace has endured. It is a massive structure, stretching some 200 metres along the riverfront. Other buildings, notably the Hermitage and the

Above: *Statue of Catherine the Great*
Below: *View of the Hermitage, the Admiralty and St Isaac's Cathedral*

St Petersburg · Russia

Hermitage Theatre, were added by Catherine the Great, a ruler whose excesses and love of power were to help to bring about revolution and the end of a dynasty.

A palpable sense of history pervades every part of the Winter Palace. It is easy to imagine the Russian royal family residing here, cocooned from the harsh realities of daily life experienced by most of their subjects. Or the monk Rasputin, who held such sway over Tsar Nicholas's wife, Alexandra, that he was poisoned the year before the dynasty fell. One can also imagine the amazement of the Bolsheviks who stormed the palace in 1917, seeing for the first time the opulence in which their rulers lived.

Opposite: *The gate from the river jetty into Peter and Paul Fortress, with the River Neva in the background*
Left: *Winter Palace*
Below: *Tikhvin cemetery*

St Petersburg · Russia

Although Communism has long since gone, the visa application process has changed little. It is time consuming and there is a lot of paperwork. A visa agency will help to smooth the process. A number of European airlines fly to St Petersburg. Alternatively, you can take the train through Europe. The city is well served by rail connections and it is possible to get a train all the way to Vladivostok or even Beijing. Try to book a central hotel – the city is big and spread out and you will maximize your sightseeing by minimizing travel time. Intourist, the old state travel company, can organize hotels and tours. The metro is an interesting experience and very efficient, but keep track of where you are – station signs are difficult to read and it is easy to miss your stop.

The Hermitage is notable among the riches of the Winter Palace, housing one of the greatest collections of art in the world – an astonishing 2.8 million exhibits. Get there early and you could have works by Monet or Picasso all to yourself.

Despite the Byzantine paperwork required to get a visa, St Petersburg is a relatively easy city to visit. Seemingly unaffected by the long years of Communism, it retains the atmosphere of imperial Russia, especially during the long hard winters when, like the tsars of old, you can seek refuge from the cold amid the warmth and grace of the Winter Palace.

Opposite above: *Pavilion Hall, Gallery 204, the Hermitage*
Opposite below: *Ceiling of the Jordan Staircase, the Hermitage*
Right: *Large Hermitage, Gallery 241*

3

HAVANA

Cuba

*A place to be experienced as much as seen, Havana lives
up to all the clichés that have characterized it for so long:
the people really do dance the rumba, drink rum and smoke
cigars. And everywhere you look, classic American cars
– Buicks, Dodges and Chevrolets – cruise along streets
that seem to have changed little since the revolution.*

The old part of the city, Habana Vieja, appears caught in a 1950s time warp. It looks like a film set, while the people who inhabit it resemble casually positioned extras: the elderly man sitting on the waterfront at sunset playing the trombone to his friend, another carrying a double bass across a square and the young woman dancing by herself to the music of the band on the terrace of El Patio restaurant. And over it all,

making the scene unmistakably Cuban, is the scent of cigar smoke.

At the centre of old Havana is the cobbled Plaza de la Catedral. Ringed on three sides by low colonial buildings, its focal point is the ornate cathedral, its Cuban baroque style reminiscent

Above: *Hotel Inglaterra and the Parque Central*
Opposite: *Buildings on the Malecón*

of melted wax on a candle. Having been spared from tourist development, the square is much as it used to be in the 1950s when pre-revolution Havana was a playground for the rich and a haunt of the Mafia. El Patio, a restaurant housed in an 18th-century mansion, has witnessed many changes in the city, and is the perfect place to watch from as the colour drains from the sky and the cathedral is floodlit. If you are lucky and there is a service on, you can look straight through the open door of the cathedral to the altar as you sit in the square.

Parts of old Havana have been renovated and restored into sanitized shadows of their former selves. The buildings in the Plaza Vieja and Mercaderes now house international shops and dollar restaurants too expensive for most

Cuban people. It is the run-down backstreets that have the real atmosphere. Everyone seems to exist outdoors, whether on a rickety balcony, in a shady courtyard or just on the front step. People laugh, talk, eat and smoke, and, most importantly, all the boys seem to play basketball – a national obsession.

Although Cuba has the highest literacy and lowest child mortality rates in all of Latin America it still has great poverty, which some attribute to 50 years of Communism and others blame squarely on the long-running US boycott. Certainly, there is limited political freedom, and everyday life can be hard. Most Cubans live in small, one- or two-room apartments, and if you look through the elaborately barred windows on the ground floor you might see the whole family

Havana · Cuba

gathered round an old TV set, watching a South American soap opera or a live baseball game. You will know which windows to look through: TVs are a rarity here, so there will often be a small crowd in the street outside watching as well.

Sometimes it seems that most of the population of Havana congregates on the Malecón at sunset. This stretch of the waterfront, lined on one side by crumbling buildings and on the other by the sea, is a magnet for people of all ages. As the once-elegant façades are bathed in golden evening light music is played, a little impromptu dancing breaks out and people sip rum cocktails as they watch the sun sink slowly into the sea.

Opposite: *Catedral de la Habana*
Above: *Cuban musicians busking in the Plaza de la Catedral*
Right: *Plaza de la Catedral*

Travel to Cuba is complicated by the travel ban imposed by the United States. The national carrier, Cubana, flies from several European and South American airports. There are also a number of flights from Cancún and Mexico City. Visas are easy to obtain and, although the US State Department forbids most of its citizens from visiting, the Cuban authorities are happy not to stamp their passports. Accommodation is plentiful in Havana, but for convenience you should stay in Habana Vieja. One of the most atmospheric hotels is the newly refurbished Ambos Mundos, where Hemingway used to stay before he bought a finca (an estate) on the island.

Above, top: *Paseo de Martí*
Above: *Door of the Capitolio Nacional*
Opposite: *Typical street in Centro de la Habana*

4

WAT PHRA KAEO
Bangkok, Thailand

*It is easy to lose yourself in the fairy-tale mystique of Wat Phra Kaeo.
Shimmering gilt towers, or stupas, vie for your attention with golden
buildings topped with soaring arched roofs of multicoloured tiles. Small
shrines give out clouds of sweet-smelling incense, and their fearsome stone
guardians tower high above your head. But this is no fantasy palace:
this is the most sacred place in Thai Buddhism – home to an Emerald
Buddha statue so precious that nations have gone to war over it.*

Above: *Gable of the Temple of the Emerald Buddha*
Opposite: *Prasat Phra Dhepbidorn (the Royal Pantheon)*

Wat Phra Kaeo is a Buddhist monastery inside the Grand Palace in central Bangkok, and although it looks shiny and new it actually dates from 1792, soon after the Thai army captured the Emerald Buddha from Laos. The most important building of Wat Phra Kaeo is the Temple of the Emerald Buddha. This massive prayer hall is built on a marble platform, and surrounded by effigies of gilded *garudas* (mythical divine birds) to ward off evil spirits. The inside of the temple is covered from floor to ceiling with incredibly detailed murals showing the life and teachings of the Buddha.

The Emerald Buddha – in reality carved jade and only 75 cm high – sits on a high altar surrounded by other Buddha images. At a small shrine just outside the Temple an almost constant stream of worshippers makes offerings of incense, food and gold leaf, before entering the prayer hall to pray.

On one side of the Wat, on another raised platform, are three stupas, the two smaller ones, encircled by statues of mystical guardians, built as memorials to the parents of King Rama I, who founded Wat Phra Kaeo. Nearby is Prasat Phra Dhepbidorn (the Royal Pantheon), where statues of past rulers are enshrined, and a library, both covered in ornate giltwork. Of interest to anyone heading on to Cambodia is a model of Angkor Wat, made almost 150 years ago.

To appreciate the peace and spirituality of Wat Phra Kaeo it is best to arrive before the coach parties. If you hurry straight to the Wat when the gates of the Grand Palace open at 8.30 a.m., you can generally have up to half an hour of total peace until you see your first camcorder. Alternatively, if you can stand the stifling heat of the afternoon, aim to arrive around 3.30 p.m. – about an hour before the palace closes. Find a shady spot and sit quietly as the crowds thin out, and for the last half hour you will be able to enjoy the place in almost

Bangkok (known to the Thais as Krung Thep, or City of Angels) is easily reached from most capital cities in the world, either on the excellent Thai Airways or on other national carriers. Traffic in Bangkok is notorious and the pollution will literally take your breath away. The most pleasant way to travel is on a river boat on the busy Chao Phraya River and there is a stop for the Grand Palace. Many of the hotels are away from the river on Silom Road but, if you can, try to get a hotel near the river. One of the most famous is the Mandarin Oriental. A much cheaper option, just some 15 minutes' walk from the Grand Palace, is the Vieng Thai near the travellers' enclave of the Khao San Road. The Grand Palace and Wat Phra Kaeo open at 8.30 a.m. Take care to observe the dress code.

complete solitude. One of the uniformed guards will gently inform you when it's time to leave.

Visitors to the Grand Palace must observe a strict dress code, which prohibits shorts and short skirts, sleeveless tops and sandals. This code is rigidly enforced and can be expanded at whim to include other 'disrespectful' items. 'Decent' clothing may be hired, but appears to date from the 1970s so it is dubious both stylistically and hygienically.

Opposite above: *Buildings of the upper terrace of Wat Phra Kaeo*
Opposite below: *Golden chedi of Phra Siratana and Phra Mondop*
Right: *Golden statue on the upper terrace at Wat Phra Kaeo*

Wat Phra Kaeo · Bangkok, Thailand

Wat Phra Kaeo · Bangkok, Thailand

Left: *Statue in front of the Temple of the Emerald Buddha*
Above top: *Guardian statue, Toskarith Ravana*
Above bottom: *Spires of Wat Phra Kaeo at sunrise*

Wat Phra Kaeo · Bangkok, Thailand

35

5

GRAND CANYON
Arizona, USA

As you stand in the cold darkness of an Arizona night, waiting for dawn, you will have no comprehension of the enormity of the landscape in front of you. In the dull early light your first view of the Grand Canyon will be a flat, almost painterly composition. Then gradually the sky turns to blue and red, and golden sunlight starts to pick out details – first the edge of the far ridge, then the tallest pinnacles inside the canyon itself.

As the sun rises higher, more is revealed. Rock formations sculpted by years of erosion are illuminated, and long, convoluted shadows are cast on to giant screens formed by cliffs.

Only when you notice details, such as a row of trees, or a flock of geese flying overhead, do you come to realize the true scale of the canyon. That far ridge might be 15 km away, and the mighty Colorado River – a mere stream viewed from above – is 1500 metres below.

Consisting of an inner and outer gorge, the canyon is some 450 km long in total, so it is impossible to try taking it all in at once. Far better to spend some time at one or two of the lookout points that punctuate the roads along the rim of the canyon and see the changing light from them.

Above: *Grandview Point*
Below: *Sunset at Yapavi Point*

Grand Canyon · Arizona, USA

From Hopi Point, a short distance from the Grand Canyon Village, you can look both ways along the canyon, getting spectacular views of the scenery and watching it change colour throughout the day. You can also see the Colorado River looking deceptively small and tranquil far below.

There are a number of trails down into the canyon. Some of the longer ones will involve camping en route but you can hike down and back up in a day on others, such as Bright Angel Trail – provided you start early enough. However, even for this shorter trail, the park authorities recommend that you break your journey at Indian Garden campsite and spread your hike over two days. Remember, it will take twice as long to walk back up the trail as it took to walk down, and it's a hard uphill slog. Those not used to exercise can hire a mule to carry them, but the ride is fairly uncomfortable. Trail-walking provides some idea of the scale of the canyon. Distances become more real as you descend, and details of the scenery unfold around

you. Soon the walls of the canyon tower above you, and you realize that the landmarks that looked so close from the rim take hours to reach.

The canyon receives over a million visitors a year, although most stay only a few hours and tend to congregate on the more accessible south rim. To avoid the worst of the crowds, visit in spring or autumn. Although it will be cold at night and in the mornings, the air is clearer and you can observe the canyon in very different conditions. The weather can change suddenly, giving clear blue skies one day and a white-out blizzard the next. However, the great depth of the canyon leads to huge temperature variations between the top and the bottom, so in the course of one day you might walk through heavy snow at the top and hot sunshine at the bottom.

Opposite above: *View from Hopi Point*
Opposite below: *View from Yaki Point*
Above: *View from Yapavi Point*

Opposite: *Sunrise at Yaki Point*
Above right: *The Colorado River from Desert View Point*
Right: *The head of Bright Angel Trail*

The nearest major airport to the Grand Canyon is at Flagstaff, a couple of hours' drive away from the south rim. If you are coming from Las Vegas you can fly directly to Grand Canyon airport at Tusayan. There is a free bus service around the park, but hiring a car is recommended as it will give you more freedom to explore. Grand Canyon Village offers a range of accommodation, but as it is all run by the same company there is little competition in pricing. The best place there is El Tovar Lodge, which is right on the rim. It gets very booked up, though, so make a reservation well in advance. The National Parks Department's website (www.nps.gov/grca) covers all aspects of the Grand Canyon.

6

TAJ MAHAL
Agra, India

*The most evocative views of the Taj Mahal
are across the Yamuna River, and getting
to the Taj is part of the magic. Although
it is quicker to take a boat across, taking
a cycle-rickshaw through the village of
Katchpura is more atmospheric. In the
cool of a pre-dawn morning, you will pass
villagers sleeping on low charpoy beds outside
their small dwellings, often passing so close
that they could reach out and touch you.*

On arriving at the river you might have to share the view with a fisherman or a small herd of water buffalo, but these merely add to the feeling of timelessness.

From across the river the Taj Mahal is best seen at sunrise, when the light turns from cold misty blue to any variation of pink, pale gold or orange. The Taj mirrors these colours, eventually reaching a soft creamy white, changing, in turn, to a blinding white in the glare of the midday sun. Those who visit at that time of day often come away disappointed. It is worth visiting at different times over several days to appreciate both the might and grace of the structure as it changes with the light. You'll have to pay to enter the Taj Mahal and grounds, but it currently costs nothing to view it from across the river.

The Taj sits on a marble platform with a marble minaret at each corner, and these minarets actually lean out slightly so that they won't fall on the main structure in the event of an earthquake. Each face of the Taj has a giant arch and is decorated with exquisite calligraphy from the

Opposite: *The Taj Mahal viewed from across the Yamuna River*
Right: *The east corner of the Taj Mahal*

Koran and ornate carvings of flowers inlaid with pietra-dura mosaics of semi-precious stones.

The Taj Mahal is set in a relaxed but formal garden complex, with pools of water leading to it from the main gate – a special view that has inspired a generation of photographers. The distance from the gate to the Taj is deceptive and the building seems to grow in both size and stature as you approach.

The Taj Mahal was built in 1632 by Emperor Shah Jahan as a mausoleum for his favourite wife, Mumtaz. Legend has it that he intended to build a duplicate Taj in black marble on the opposite side of the river as his own tomb. In recent years the ruins of foundations and gardens have been discovered there, which seems to support this theory, but the truth will probably never be known. Shah Jahan was overthrown by his son and spent his last days locked up in Agra Fort, just down the river from the Taj.

Above: *Detail of a door in the pedestal of the Taj Mahal*
Right: *The Taj Mahal from across the Yamuna River at sunrise*

Taj Mahal · Agra, India

Agra can be reached by plane or fast train from New Delhi, although the latter has a
reputation for pickpockets. All the rooms in the new luxury Amarvilas hotel in Agra look
out on the Taj Mahal so uniquely, you don't have to pay a premium for good views if you
stay there. The bustling streets of Taj Ganj, just outside the main gate, were once the
home of the craftsmen who constructed the Taj. It is now a backpacker's ghetto with very
cheap accommodation. Some of the best views can be had from the roof-top restaurant of
the Shanti Lodge. Other attractions include the fort in Agra, which has good views down
the Yamuna River to the Taj, and also the deserted city of Fatehpur Sikri a few hours away.

Above: *Detail of the Dome*
Opposite above: *Agra Fort with the Taj Mahal behind*
Opposite below: *Western mosque flanking the Taj Mahal*

Taj Mahal · Agra, India

7

EILEAN DONAN CASTLE
Scotland

*Situated at the meeting point of three sea lochs – Loch Alsh,
Loch Duich and Loch Long – and looking west to the Isle
of Skye, the castle of Eilean Donan, or island of Donan,
combines spectacular location and colourful history in a
way that makes it everything a British castle should be.*

The MacKenzie clan held Eilean Donan until the 16th century, during which time it survived feuds with the McLeods and the MacDonalds. It also saw a great deal of action during the 17th and 18th centuries when Jacobites – supporters of the deposed King James VII of Scotland (II of England) – rose up against the English in attempts to take the throne for him and his heirs. In the spring of 1719 the Jacobites garrisoned 46 Spanish soldiers in Eilean Donan. On 10 May three government frigates bombarded the castle. The government force accepted the garrison's surrender and blew up what was not already in ruins with the help of 343 barrels of gunpowder.

Above: *Eilean Donan Castle from the south*
Opposite: *Eilean Donan Castle*

Given its long and often violent history, it is not surprising that the castle of Eilean Donan has been rebuilt a number of times. The earliest structure on this site was built in medieval times as a defence against the Vikings, and the most recent rebuilding was by the MacRae-Gilstrap family between 1912 and 1932.

The approach to the castle is understated, and crosses a graceful bridge that was added at the time of the last rebuilding. From this bridge there are views of the lochs, the nearby village of Dornie and the mountains of Skye. Although its outline slightly resembles a broken tooth the castle looks good from almost any angle, set as it is within a fragrant and typically Highland landscape of heather and wild flowers.

Opposite: *The castle approach*
Above top: *The bridge to the castle*

Eilean Donan Castle · Scotland

Eilean Donan Castle is in a fairly remote location 16 km from the bridge to the Isle of Skye. Driving from Glasgow takes about 7 hours, primarily on the A82, but the road passes through some essential scenery, including Ben Nevis, Glen Coe, Loch Lochy and Glen Shiel. Driving from Edinburgh also takes 7 hours, and from Inverness 3 hours. The nearby village of Dornie is small and has limited hotel and bed-and-breakfast capacity, especially in the summer months, so booking ahead is advisable. The road leading up the hill behind Dornie has good views above the castle, especially at sunset.

Its severe beauty, however, cannot disguise the fact that the castle's primary function has always been defence. There is no retreat from an island battle, and the finality of Eilean Donan's position certainly contributes to its atmosphere.

The end of the bridge is protected by the battlements of the bastion and a wall that extends outwards from the main castle. A doorway leads into the courtyard, which has a sea wall that looks out on to the lochs. Steps lead up to the door of the keep and into the billeting room. Above is the most impressive room, the banqueting hall, complete with beams made from Douglas fir from British Columbia, given by the Canadian MacRaes during the rebuilding. The hall also has a huge fireplace decorated with coats of arms and a table believed to be from one of Admiral Nelson's ships.

At low tide the island is fringed with seaweed and tide pools, but at high tide its exposed position gives it a sense of defiance and it is possible to imagine enemy ships sailing down Loch Alsh, or besieging troops planning to fight their way across to the castle.

Reflected in the waters of the loch and framed by mountains, the castle is now a place of dreams rather than drama.

Above: *The billeting room*
Opposite above: *The banqueting hall*
Opposite below: *Eilean Donan Castle at night*

Eilean Donan Castle · Scotland

8

THE ALHAMBRA
Granada, Spain

*Overlooking Granada, the Alhambra presents a hard and unyielding
face to the world, its square towers displaying martial symmetry.
This severity is softened when you approach from the back, as
terraces of ornate gardens, interspersed with pools of running water,
seek to emulate the shady, cool gardens of the Koranic heaven.*

After the heat and dryness of North Africa the Moors must have thought they had reached heaven when they conquered Granada. The Sierra Nevada, snow-capped for much of the year, provided the conquerors with water for the fountains and pools that helped to make this corner of Spain paradise on Earth.

The Alhambra is a product of the wars between Christianity and Islam. The Moors of North Africa conquered Spain in 711, but by the beginning of

Below: *Patio de los Leones*
Opposite: *Cloister at one end of Patio de los Arrayanes, Casa Real*

the 13th century their influence had weakened and their 'kingdom' – just a few independent Muslim states in what is now Andalusia – was under pressure from Christian reconquistas. Prince Ibn al-Ahmar, who was driven south from Saragossa, decided to create a new capital at Granada, and began building the fortifications that would keep it safe. For over 200 years the kingdom prospered, and subsequent rulers added to and refined the Alhambra. It was a period of peace that came at a price, however. During this time the Christian kings of Spain were in the ascendancy, and Granada was left in peace only because the Moors paid tributes and sometimes sent troops to fight on the side of the Christians against other, more troublesome, Muslim city states.

At the end of the 15th century the battlements of the Alhambra were called into use when the army of Catholic rulers Ferdinand and Isabella laid siege to Granada. Seven months later this last Muslim stronghold in Spain gave way, and it has remained in Spanish hands ever since.

The Alhambra · Granada, Spain

Typical of Moorish architecture, the palace has a façade that is both commanding and utilitarian, yet hidden within its defensive walls is decoration of enduring beauty. The Alhambra consists of three main parts: the Alcazaba, or fortress; the Generalife, which was the summer palace and actually lies outside the main defensive walls; and the Casa Real, or Royal Palace. The last of these is without doubt the most beautiful part of the Alhambra, many of its rooms decorated with colourful tiles or richly carved stonework, the patterns based on stylized quotes from the Koran.

Within some of these rooms you can still see the fountains or pools of water so prized by the Moors. Numerous small windows overlook shady gardens or the small white houses of the Albaicin

Above: *The Alhambra floodlit at dusk with the Sierra Nevada behind*
Opposite: *Gardens of the Generalife*
Left: *Intricate Moorish decoration*

The Alhambra · Granada, Spain

district, the old Moorish quarter, parts of which are as old as the Alhambra itself.

Spring is a beautiful time to visit, with clear warm days and cool nights. The trees are newly green, the gardens are in flower and the Sierra Nevada, still snow-capped, stands watch over the city. Even better, the Casa Real is not crowded and you can generally get in without queueing or waiting for a slot, as you must in the height of summer, when all the timed entrance tickets are often allocated within an hour of the ticket office opening.

You might also be able to get a room at the Parador de San Francisco, a luxury, state-run hotel in a converted monastery within the gardens of the Alhambra – a tranquil retreat in the evenings when the crowds have gone.

There are many vantage points around the city from which you can get a different perspective on the Alhambra. From the Mirador San Cristobel you will see the Alcazaba against the backdrop of the Sierra Nevada. Walk through the rambling, cobbled streets of Albaicin to the Mirador de San Nicolas and you will see wonderful sunsets that bathe the Alhambra in glowing red light. From the top of the Sacromonte (the old gypsy quarter, where some gypsies still live in caves carved into the hillside) you will see how the Alhambra towers over the town from its perfect defensive position. And from the hill above the Generalife you can appreciate how much the gardens and water terraces contribute to the Alhambra. Also visible is the massive Palacio de Carlos V, built in the 16th century, after the Christian conquest, on the site of many lesser Moorish buildings. The grounds of this palace are so large that bullfights were once held in the courtyard.

Granada is easily reached by road from Seville or Málaga, two international airports that are well served by the Iberia airline from most parts of Europe. While the Alhambra is seen to advantage from many viewpoints around the city, you can enjoy it at close quarters by staying in its gardens at the luxurious Parador de San Francisco. However, you should book well in advance for the privilege, even in the low season.

Opposite: *Bronze eagle on the exterior of the Palacio de Carlos V*

Right: *Moorish decoration*

Below: *Tha Alhambra seen from the hill behind the Generalife*

9

AITUTAKI
Cook Islands

No artist's palette could ever conceive of a more perfect, more luminescent turquoise than that of the lagoon of Aitutaki, arguably the most beautiful in the world. Triangular in shape, the lagoon is formed by an atoll that rises some 4000 metres from the base of the Pacific Ocean. Within the lagoon is Aitutaki itself, the main island of the group, and a number of volcanic and coral motus, or islets.

The outer rim of the lagoon acts as a natural barrier that calms the sometimes rough waters of the southern Pacific ocean. The meeting point of the waters is marked by a constant white fringe of breaking waves, but the lagoon itself has a glassy smooth surface only occasionally broken by a solitary breakaway ripple. Its waters are remarkably clear, and every detail of its flat, sandy base is perfectly visible, however deep the water. Turtles, rays and even giant clams can often be seen.

Each motu has its own distinct character, and one of the best ways to witness this is by taking

Above: *The lagoon from the air*
Opposite: *Moturakau Island*

a lagoon cruise. The most well-known motu is Tapuaetai (One Foot Island). Typically tropical, with a stand of palm trees perched on a thin sliver of dazzling white sand, it is the only inhabited motu. Alongside its small bar and shop is a post office where you can get your passport stamped to show that you have been to paradise.

The tiny island of Moturakau was chosen as the location for a British reality TV series. It takes only about 10 minutes to walk around, and is another haven of white sandy beaches and palm trees. Here some of the trees lean so far out over the sea that they are almost horizontal.

The newest of the motus is Honeymoon Island, which is tucked away in a shallower part of the lagoon. While it hasn't been around long enough to grow any trees, a number of bushes provide

Opposite: *Giant clams in the clear waters of the lagoon*
Above: *The lagoon*
Right: *Beach on Akitua Islet*

shelter for a large population of nesting terns. Every bush seems to have a fluffy white chick crouched beneath it, waiting for its parents to return with food. The restless Pacific carries windfall coconuts from other motus and washes them up on the beaches of Honeymoon Island, so it might not be too long before the first palm tree takes root.

The 15 tiny islands that make up the Cook Islands archipelago have a total land area of just 236 square kilometres but are spread over a vast area of ocean. Their inhabitants are of Polynesian descent, and the total population is around 18,000. On Aitutaki everyone appears to know each other, and no task seems so important that they won't take the time to say hello to passers-by. Try walking anywhere and people will stop to offer you a lift.

Others, apart from tourists, are attracted to Aitutaki – as indicated by the captain's languid announcement on the flight from Rarotonga: 'Passengers on the left of the plane, if you look out of the window, you can see Aitutaki, whereas passengers on the right can see a humpback whale and her calf.'

For such an out-of-the-way place, Aitutaki has a significant claim to fame: Captain Bligh arrived here on the Bounty in 1789, shortly before the famous mutiny. He returned in 1792 and introduced the pawpaw to the island, where it remains one of the most important crops.

Opposite above: *Beach on Akitua Islet*
Opposite below left: *Dead starfish*
Opposite below right: *Hermit crab*

Air Rarotonga flies from Rarotonga (the capital island in the Cook Islands archipelago) to Aitutaki up to five times a day. It is possible to visit Aitutaki on a day trip from Rarotonga, but it is much better to stay there for at least a couple of days. Accommodation varies from the luxurious Aitutaki Pacific Resort to inexpensive communal beach huts. Any of the hotels will be able to book you on one of the lagoon cruises. Visit www.cook-islands.com for more information on all aspects of the Cook Islands.

Aitutaki · Cook Islands

10
PYRAMID OF KUKULCÁN
Mexico

*Sitting at the centre of the ancient Mayan site of
Chichén Itzá on the Yucatán peninsula in Mexico, the
pyramid of Kukulcán has a pleasing symmetry and an
imposing bulk, but perhaps its true majesty lies in the
secrets of its construction – over 1000 years ago.*

The pyramid is a giant calendar. It consists of
nine levels faced with a total of 52 panels – the
number of years in the Mayan–Toltec cycle. The
staircases on each face of the pyramid have
364 steps. Add the square platform at the top,
and you have 365 – the number of days in the
solar year. Most impressively, at the spring and
autumn equinoxes the shadow cast by the sun
on the northern staircase appears to cause a
massively long 'snake' to crawl down the building
and link with the stone serpent's head at the foot
of the staircase.

The pyramid of Kukulcán has other secrets
too. Hidden deep within it is another, much older
pyramid. A small door takes you to a narrow
passage that appears to run up what would
have been the outside of the original structure.
Cramped and oppressive, it leads to the original
sanctuary, where a large chac-mool – the
characteristic reclining Mayan figure – and a
jaguar-shaped throne are for ever entombed,
the jade inlay of the big cat's coat shining dimly
through the gloom.

You will have to get up early to appreciate
Kukulcán properly because by 10.30 a.m. it is
swarming with visitors. If you are among the first
through the gate at 8.30 in the morning, you
should manage an hour of near-solitude. A good
way to achieve this is to stay at the Mayaland
Hotel, just a few metres from the quiet east
gate. Here you will be so close that you can see
the ruins of the ossuary, or bone sanctuary,
silhouetted by the setting sun and filling the
doorway of the hotel bar.

From the top of the pyramid the whole site
seems to be completely surrounded by a sea of
trees stretching as far as the eye can see, and
obliterating almost all signs of human life. Only
the tops of some of the lesser ruins and the open
grassed ceremonial area are visible.

A number of other ruins make up the
ceremonial area of Chichén Itzá, including

*Opposite above: The stone serpent's
head near Kukulcán's pyramid*
Opposite below: Detail of cladding on Kukulcán's pyramid

Pyramid of Kukulcán · Mexico

Pyramid of Kukulcán · Mexico

the Temple of the Warriors, a large structure surrounded by intricately carved stone pillars and topped with a reclining chac-mool. Sadly, visitors are no longer allowed to mount the steps to see this statue, so you will have to make do with looking down on it from the top of the pyramid of Kukulcán.

The other most impressive structure is the ball court, once the scene of a complicated game in which teams of players attempted to pass a rubber ball through a stone hoop high up on the wall using only their elbows, knees and hips. It often took hours to achieve this and consequently the game was won on the first score.

The pyramid is visible from many of the outlying structures on the site, which gives you the chance to appreciate its harmonious proportions from a number of perspectives: through dense trees, from the top of carved pillars and even appearing between the jaws of a stone serpent's head.

Every evening there is a sound and light show at the complex, which is included in the ticket price. Although the show is garish, it's worth attending

on nights when there is a full moon because if you linger afterwards you will get a unique view of Kukulcán's pyramid illuminated only by the moon, and glowing in its incandescent light.

Previous spread: *Kukulcán's pyramid,*
North staircase on Kukulcán's pyramid
Above: *Head of chac-mool*
Below: *Observatory in a sea of trees*
Opposite: *Wall of skulls on the Tzompantli, a sacrificial altar*

Pyramid of Kukulcán · Mexico

The airport nearest to Chichén Itzá is at Cancún, and the site is reachable by bus or hire car. If you are staying at the Mayaland Hotel you should get off at the park gate and walk through the site. Many tourists visit Chichén Itzá on a day trip, but you should aim to stay at least overnight so that you can see the site in the quiet mornings and afternoons. The interior of Kukulcán's pyramid is only open in the middle of the day so you will have to brave the crowds at least once.

11

VENICE

Italy

*No city is more romantic than Venice, and no sight more
essentially Venetian than gondolas bobbing on a misty Molo,
the waterfront where the Piazza San Marco meets the lagoon.
In the very early morning the square is quiet, with only a few
commuters disturbing the handful of pigeons that strut imperiously
on its worn flagstones. Soon the place will be thronged with both
tourists and birds, but for now you can be virtually alone.*

Piazza San Marco has been at the centre of
the city since it was first constructed in the
16th century, although some of the buildings
around it date from much earlier. At one end
lies the Basilica di San Marco, construction of
which began almost 1000 years ago. Squat and
strangely shaped, its domed roof looks more
Islamic than Christian when seen from the soaring
heights of the adjacent campanile, or bell tower.
At sunset the façade of the basilica seems to
come alive as the mosaics, and even the stone
itself, glow in the warm evening light.

Stretching from San Marco down to the
waterfront is the Gothic white edifice of the
Palazzo Ducale, or Doge's Palace. The doges ruled
the city from AD 697 until Napoleon's troops
deposed the last of them in 1797. Although
peppered with moralistic statues and carvings that
depict such things as the fall of Adam and Eve, and
a drunken Noah, the palace is best appreciated
from afar, as it would have been by visitors arriving
by sea in the days of the doges. Seen from a
boat on the lagoon, or even from the top of the

Above: *Relief of Adam and Eve on the
corner of the Palazzo Ducale*

Opposite: *Gondolas moored in front of the
church of Santa Maria della Salute*

campanile on the island of San Giorgio, the façade combines elegance with a feeling of fantasy.

If the doges wished to portray an impression of piety with the outside of their palace, the inside shows a much more worldly extravagance. Room after room is decorated with the finest gilding and paintings, including works by Titian and Tintoretto.

The doges were responsible for the judicial side of Venetian life, and many condemned people were led across the two-lane Bridge of Sighs to the prisons opposite.

Although not, strictly speaking, connected to the Piazza San Marco, the Grand Canal is linked with it. A lazy, sweeping 'S' shape, it cuts through the city, defining it almost as much as the piazza does. The end of the canal opens into the lagoon where it meets the piazza, and the waterfront here is lined with the ubiquitous gondolas.

As all roads in Venice seem to lead to Piazza San Marco – virtually every street or alley junction has a signpost pointing in that direction – so all canals seem to lead to the Grand Canal. Now used mainly by tourists, gondolas still glide past the palazzos that line its sides.

Venice can be cold and damp during the winter, but this is a perfect time to visit. There are far fewer visitors, hotel prices are lower and, if you are lucky, you might even be there when the water floods Piazza San Marco, forcing locals and tourists on to raised walkways to keep their feet dry. Even in the winter you can experience blue skies and amazingly clear light.

A perfect winter day in Venice has to end with a warming hot chocolate or a typically Venetian spritz cocktail (white wine, lemon peel, a bitter aperitif and seltzer) at Caffè Florian. Founded in 1720, this elegant café, once patronized by Byron and Goethe, is decorated with mirrors and murals cracked by years of damp sea air.

Above: *Façade of buildings around Piazza San Marco*
Opposite above left: *Palazzo Ducale*
Opposite above right: *Façade of the Basilica di San Marco*
Opposite below: *Piazzetta San Marco*

Venice · Italy

Venice · Italy

Venice · Italy

Left: *Palazzo Ducale from the top of the campanile*
Above: *Palazzo Ducale*

From Marco Polo airport you can catch a vaporetto (water bus) or water taxi that drops you off at the Molo. Accommodation is expensive and can be hard to find in the peak summer months. The industrial town of Mestre is a short train ride away and offers cheaper options. The Regina and Europa Hotel is a luxury establishment in a converted palazzo, overlooking the mouth of the Grand Canal. A network of vaporetti plies the main canals and is a good way to get around. Otherwise, just walk and enjoy the experience of getting lost.

12

DEAD VLEI

Sossusvlei National Park, Namibia

In the parched landscape of the Namib Desert, the golden-orange light of dawn starts by illuminating the very tips of the dead camelthorn trees that point skeletal branches at the lightening sky. It then moves down their trunks and onwards, just as it has done every morning of their 600-year existence, until it reaches the drought-crazed white surface of Dead Vlei. Then everything appears to speed up, as the sunlight pushes aside the shroud of shadow and sweeps across the pan of the former lake. The contrast between the cracked white of Dead Vlei and the red sand dunes that surround it is stark. There is literally a hard line where one finishes and the other begins.

A vlei is a lake pan, and there are three in the Sossusvlei National Park. Although Dead Vlei is smaller than the more famous Sossusvlei that gave the park its name, it is more atmospheric and has a more impressive location. (The third is the even smaller Hidden Vlei.)

Sossusvlei is part of the great Namib Desert from which Namibia takes its name. As public transport links to the park aren't good, travellers generally find it much easier to stay at one of the luxury camps that run their own transport into the park. If your budget won't stretch to this, cheaper accommodation is available near the park gate at Sesriem.

Above: *Dunes in the valley of the Tsauchab River*
Opposite: *Hiking across the ridge of Dune 45*

Driving across the desert terrain is difficult. There is a car park for four-wheel-drive vehicles about 4 km away from Sossusvlei. However, drivers of two-wheel-drive vehicles must use a car park situated along a dirt track about 60 km from the park gate and take a shuttle bus to the four-wheel-drive car park. It's then a hard, 20-minute uphill hike to Dead Vlei.

Despite the almost complete lack of water in the area – Sossusvlei was last flooded in 1997, but Dead Vlei has not flooded in living memory – you can still see some forms of life. Gawky ostriches

stalk around, and oryx stand motionless in the heat haze, as if waiting for the day to cool before they deign to move. On a smaller scale, look down at the sand and you will often see the erratic trails of beetles.These creatures spend most of their time burrowed in the sand, and survive by tilting their bodies to catch the morning dew that sometimes sweeps in from the sea many kilometres away on the Atlantic coast, their heads down to catch and drink the condensation that forms on their hard shells.

Above: *Shadows sweeping across Dead Vlei at sunrise*

Dead Vlei · Sossusvlei National Park, Namibia

The national park is also famous for its sand dunes, which are reputed to be the tallest in the world: Big Daddy, the tallest at Sossusvlei, is over 300 metres high. The dunes are a deep red colour, which is especially intense when lit by the rising or setting sun.

You should definitely try to climb at least one of the dunes, but make sure you take plenty of water with you, as it's a hot and draining experience. From the top you will have spectacular views of the desert, with endless series of dunes stretching out in front of you – a sight that is both humbling and awe-inspiring.

While you are visiting Namibia you should aim to take in the Skeleton Coast, a desolate stretch of the Atlantic seaboard where shipwrecks, whale bones and even the occasional lion can be found on the beach.

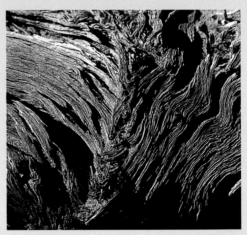

Above left: *Camelthorn tree in Dead Vlei*
Above: *Camelthorn tree*
Opposite: *Dunes looming over camelthorn trees in the Tsauchab River valley*

Dead Vlei · Sossusvlei National Park, Namibia

Sossusvlei can be reached by road from the Namibian capital, Windhoek, or from Cape Town – a long drive across the South African border. Accommodation close to the park entrance at Sesriem is limited, but there are several luxury camps and lodges about an hour from the main park gate. The desert is best appreciated from the top of one of the dunes, but if you decide to climb one do make sure you take more water than you think you'll need. Have plenty of cash, too – petrol stations in Namibia do not take credit cards.

Dead Vlei · Sossusvlei National Park, Namibia

13

IGUASSU FALLS

Brazil and Argentina

If you were to design the perfect waterfall then Iguassu would have to be it. Straddling the border between Brazil and Argentina, where it is known as Saltos do Iguaçu and Cataratas del Iguazú respectively, it comprises a range of cataracts.

One such is the Devil's Throat (Garganta del Diablo), which has a classic horseshoe shape and drops into a deep chasm. A walkway runs from the Argentinian side to the edge of the cataract, allowing you to stare directly at the wall of water as it drops into the void below.

The Santa Maria Cataract, which falls over the Brazilian side of the border, is interrupted halfway

Above: *Spray over Iguassu Falls at sunrise*
Opposite: *The Devil's Throat (Garganta del Diablo) and the top of Salto Santa Maria*

down by a plateau. Here the water is dotted with moss-encrusted rocks and spanned by a walkway that provides views up and down the falls and is festooned with rainbows.

Both walkways provide an experience for all the senses: the endless rushing sound that grows to a roar as you approach, the sheets of cooling spray as you get closer, and the buffeting winds, caused by the great volume of water pushing the air out of the way.

The whole waterfall stretches for a couple of kilometres and includes many other cataracts, some approachable only by boat, others visible only from an island that sits in the middle of the river above the falls. Iguassu is surrounded on both sides by verdant rainforest, which has been made into two national parks.

Uniquely for the sights in this book, an early start is not required as the sunlight barely hits the lower parts of the falls until an hour or two after dawn.

While most of Iguassu is in Argentina, some of the best views are on the Brazilian side, especially at sunset. It is a simple process to cross over for the day as travel agents on both sides offer inexpensive trips.

Opposite above: Salto Tres Mosqueteros on the Argentinian side
Opposite centre: The Argentinian side in the setting sun
Opposite below: The Argentinian side of the falls
Above: The Devil's Throat (Garganta del Diablo)

Iguassu Falls · Brazil and Argentina

The Brazilian side of the border is probably the least developed, and those seeking seclusion should consider staying at the Tropical das Cataratas eco-hotel. Built in a Portuguese colonial style, with some rooms overlooking part of the waterfall, and a clock tower from which you can watch the sunset, the hotel is actually inside the national park. Although there are signs warning against jaguars and snakes you can stroll down to the falls at night, when the dull roar seems even louder, and you might just be able to make out the spray in the moonlight.

If you can combine your visit with a full moon there are special night visits open to everybody, and the moonlight is bright enough to make out many details of the falls.

There are flights to Foz do Iguaçu, the town on the Brazilian side of the falls, from both Rio de Janeiro and Saõ Paulo. Though many people do day trips from these cities it is better to stay for at least a couple of days to allow time to visit the Argentinian side. This is very easy – most local hotels arrange trips – and you won't even need a visa. You can also raft on the river, explore the surrounding forest and even take a helicopter ride. The Tropical das Cataratas hotel on the less-developed Brazilian side will give you privileged access to the falls – especially on Monday mornings when the park is officially closed to non-guests.

Iguassu Falls · Brazil and Argentina

Iguassu Falls · Brazil and Argentina

14

PETRA

Jordan

The city of Petra was carved from red sandstone in the 3rd century BC by nomadic Arabs known as Nabataeans. The only entrance is through a siq – a long, narrow gorge. This channel, eroded by thousands of years of floods, forms a twisting and convoluted pathway through solid rock that looms up to 100 metres on either side.

At some points along its 1.2-km length the *siq* is wide enough for the sunlight to flood in and lift the dark and oppressive atmosphere, but at others it is no wider than a couple of metres, and the walls appear to close above your head. An early morning visit can be an eerie experience, with just the wind whistling through the gorge and the strangely tinny echo of your own footsteps.

At one time the *siq* would have been crowded with camel trains laden with wealth, and even the invading Romans, who finally conquered the city in AD 106, would have had to fight their way down its entire length.

Rounding the final and narrowest corner of the *siq* you are confronted by the towering façade of Al Khazneh (the treasury), which is the enduring image of the city. Although the carvings on the treasury have been damaged by Bedouin, who once lived among the deserted ruins and used the statues for target practice, there is still much to be seen. This includes the large urn on the top of the structure, that the Bedouin shot at in the belief that it contained the lost treasure of King Solomon.

Excavations taking place in front of the treasury seem to indicate that it had another storey below the current structure, which is now buried under debris washed down by the annual flash floods that created the *siq*. The treasury is fully bathed in sunlight for a couple of hours from around

Opposite: *The royal tombs seen from the High Place of Sacrifice*

Right: *Looking down the* siq *to Al Khazneh (the treasury)*

9.30 in the morning, but looks pinker and more atmospheric when in shadow. A good, though officially unsanctioned, view can be had by climbing the rock face to the right of the *siq*, to a ledge level with the top of the treasury.

All the great façades, including the treasury, are, in fact, tombs. Dwellings have long since disappeared, but you can still see the 7000-seat theatre carved out of rock, and a temple built by the Romans when they governed the city. There is also a major stretch of Nabatean road running past an old market area that would once have been thronged with shoppers and merchants trading goods and treasures brought to Petra from all over the Middle East.

Opposite: *The façade of Al Khazneh (the treasury)*
Right: *Camels in front of the treasury with the siq behind*
Below: *Roman temple*

It is no wonder that, tucked away in the middle of the desert, the city remained hidden and forgotten for 300 years after it was finally deserted, with only Bedouin living in its caves and tombs. It was 'rediscovered' for the West by Johann Burckhardt in 1812.

Although the Bedouin no longer live in the city they are still much in evidence, having been given sole rights to the various tourist concessions on the site in return for moving out to a nearby village.

Petra is huge, and you will need a good few days to do it justice, especially if you are planning to visit some of the more outlying places, such as the monastery up in the adjacent hills. A good way to appreciate the size of Petra is to climb the steep steps to the High Place of Sacrifice, where you can see over most of the city and watch as the sun slides behind the camel-shaped mountain on the far side of the valley, before making your way back to your hotel through the rapidly darkening *siq*.

Below: *Eroded carving of a man with a camel in the siq*
Opposite left: *Interior of the treasury*
Opposite right: *Building on the street of façades*

Petra is just a few hours' drive from the Jordanian capital Amman and is easily reached by bus or by car. There are a number of hotels in Petra, but the five-star Movenpick is just a few minutes from the site gate, making an early start a little easier. There are places inside the site that sell food and drinks but you should carry adequate water with you to avoid dehydration. The site is open from dawn till 6 p.m., although you can often linger longer to see the sunset. Passes for one, two or three days are available from the visitor centre. You can also hire a guide there.

15

COLLEGE FJORD

Alaska, USA

*Face towards one of the 16 glaciers that carve their way
down the Chugach Mountains of College Fjord and even
though the ambient temperature is low you will be able to feel
a wave of cold air coming from these solid walls of ice.*

College Fjord was discovered in 1898 by an expedition looking for a way to get to the goldfields of the Klondike without having to pass through the Yukon. The fjord runs for 30 km and the glaciers in it are named after American Ivy League colleges. The furthest point is Harvard Glacier, one of the few that is still advancing towards the cold waters of the Gulf of Alaska. Although others are still grinding down steep-sided valleys towards the sea, they are melting faster than they are moving, which gives them the appearance of retreating.

The most convenient way to reach College Fjord is on a cruise, which will generally take in Prince William Sound to the south-east, and for the more adventurous there are opportunities to kayak in close to the glaciers. Aim to be up for sunrise, when the clouds that often flow over the Chugach Mountains and sometimes blanket the waters of the fjord are stained orange and purple by the early morning light.

The colour of the ice ranges from a clean, stark white at the top of a mountain through to a range of turquoise and blue at the hard ice face. (No wonder the languages of many native peoples

Above: *Fog over College Fjord with the
Chugach Mountains in the background*
Opposite: *Glacier flowing down from the Chugach Mountains*

College Fjord · Alaska, USA

from cold regions have many different words for ice and snow.) The glaciers are also stained by earth and rocks picked up as they carve their way down the steep-sided valleys. They move in geological time and there is a distinct line at the point where the rock and forest on the mountain meet the snaking ice flows.

The size and scale of the fjord and glaciers are difficult to estimate. Viewed from a ship the solid walls of ice meeting the sea seem perhaps as high as a house, but in reality they could be 10 times that. The compression of scale also obscures the structure of the glaciers. From afar, they look merely ridged and pitted, but as you get closer you will be able to make out great cracks, sheer spikes and deep ravines formed by the incredible pressure as millions of tonnesof ice scour down the mountains, gouging out rock on either side. As each wall of ice reaches the sea it plunges into the water, causing large chunks to break off and float across the fjord. This process is known as 'calving'. Some of the falling chunks can be the size of a house, and the noise of them splitting from the glacier and then hitting the water is phenomenal. At sunrise and sunset these chunks of ice catch the light, making the sea look like a giant sheet of cracked and pitted glass.

For such a seemingly inhospitable environment there is a surprising amount of wildlife in College

College Fjord's remote location means it is practically impossible to reach it by any means other than a cruise ship. Cruise lines such as Norwegian Cruise Line or Princess Cruises make a seven-night one-way journey from either Seattle or Vancouver up to Seward (which is 3 hours from Anchorage), usually stopping at Ketchikan, Juneau, Skagway and Glacier Bay. There are also round trips from Seattle or Vancouver, or one-way cruises southbound from Seward. The best time to go is between June and August, as the winters are long and bitter.

Fjord. If you are particularly lucky you might see stark black-and-white orcas on your cruise, or even pure white beluga whales, although you are more likely to see sea otters or seals in the icy waters.

Opposite left: *Glacier flowing down from the Chugach Mountains*
Opposite right: *A glacier terminus at College Fjord*
Below: *Orcas (killer whales)*
Overleaf: *Glacier winding down from the Chugach Mountains*

16

KARNAK TEMPLE
Luxor, Egypt

Karnak Temple is a lasting tribute to the ancient Egyptian pharaohs' quest for immortality. And as a powerful religious institution it is arguably more representative of life in ancient Egypt than the Giza pyramids which, despite their impressive size, are ultimately tombs for the dead rulers of the Old Kingdom. The temple's influence, which lasted for more than 1300 years, was central to the power of numerous New Kingdom pharaohs, including Seti I and Rameses II.

The Great Hypostyle Hall, which is more than 3500 years old, covers an area of 6000 square metres and contains a forest of 136 stone pillars, each 23 metres tall and 15 metres in circumference. Many of these have been extensively renovated, but are still covered with deeply carved hieroglyphics and elaborate bas-relief depictions of Egyptian gods, especially Amun to whom this precinct of the temple is dedicated. Some of the pillars still

Below: *The Precinct of Amun reflected in the Sacred Lake*
Opposite: *Statues in front of the seventh pylon of the Precinct of Amun*

bear traces of the original colouring, dating back to around 1300 BC.

In the days of the pharaohs the whole of the hall would have been roofed over, and the remains of some of the lintels that supported the roof can still be seen. The interior would have been in semi-darkness, punctuated by shafts of light from grilled windows along the central aisle. It is easy to imagine processions of priests passing through its hallowed halls, and even Pharaohs coming to admire the bas-reliefs of gods in their own image.

The precinct of Amun is the largest and most complete of the three enclosures that make up Karnak Temple. The other enclosures, the Temple of Mut and the Precinct of Mont, are largely ruins. Whilst the Great Hypostyle Hall is Amun's most impressive structure, there is a great deal more to

see in the complex. From the entrance, an avenue of ram-headed sphinxes leads up to the first pylon, a 43-metre-high wall with a gap in the middle to allow entry. Inside the courtyard beyond the wall is a colossal statue of Rameses II, and a small temple devoted to Rameses III. There are a number of sphinxes outside this temple and more tall statues inside. Beyond the next pylon lie the pillars of the Hypostyle Hall, and beyond that the rest of Karnak Temple, which you could easily spend a couple of days exploring. I would recommend employing the services of a local guide, if only to save you from

Opposite: *The Tuthmosid obelisk and pillars in the Great Hypostyle Hall*

Above: *Defaced bas-reliefs in a sanctuary in the Precinct of Amun*

Karnak Temple · Luxor, Egypt

the temple guards and their constant demands for baksheesh, a small tip.

Karnak tends to get very crowded during the day, but if you arrive as it opens at six in the morning it is often deserted. Take the correct entrance money as the gate seldom has change at this time, and leave by 9 a.m. to avoid the worst of the crowds. If you can cope with the afternoon heat, it's worth returning after 3 p.m. when the tour groups have left and the temple is quiet again. You can sometimes use the same ticket in the morning and afternoon, especially if you mention at the gate when you leave that you will be returning.

You can return to town by walking along the Avenue of Sphinxes, once the route of a procession in honour of Amun. Nowadays, many of the sphinxes are missing and the avenue disappears briefly on the outskirts of Luxor. It can be picked up again at the back gate to Luxor Temple, where it joins a more impressive avenue of sphinxes linking the temples of Karnak and Luxor just as they were linked in the time of the pharaohs.

Right: *Pillars in the Great Hypostyle Hall*

Opposite left: *A sanctuary in the Precinct of Amun*

Opposite above right: *The feet of the colossus of Rameses II in the Precinct of Amun*

Opposite below right: *Bas-relief on the exterior wall of the Great Hypostyle Hall*

Luxor is easily reached by internal flights from Cairo or you can catch the very comfortable night train from the capital. The most famous hotel in Luxor is the old Winter Palace in the centre of town, but the Nile Hilton Hotel is more convenient for Karnak. Official guides can be hired from the ticket office, but agree the price first. Taxis are very cheap but, as with everything in Egypt, haggle hard. You can also take a horse-drawn calèche, but choose only healthy-looking horses and stop the driver from galloping them. Do not leave Luxor without visiting the Valleys of the Kings and Queens across the Nile.

Karnak Temple · Luxor, Egypt

17

RIO DE JANEIRO
Brazil

*The mountain of Corcovado, topped by a
32-metre statue of Christ the Redeemer facing
out over Guanabara Bay, has to be the great
enduring image of Rio de Janeiro. From up
here, on a clear day, you can see almost
the whole city, from the downtown business
district to the internationally famous beaches
of Ipanema and Copacabana. It also has one
of the best views of Sugar Loaf Mountain,
another of the city's great landmarks.*

Rio is arguably the most stunning harbour city in
the world, pipping both Sydney and Hong Kong
in my estimation. While the last two are amazing
in their own way, Rio has the advantage of being
built on a series of hills, some of which are still
covered by virgin forest, and looks out over the
most beautiful natural scenery of the granite
islands in Guanabara Bay. Corcovado, set within
a park that opens at 8 a.m., can be reached either
by taxi or by a creaking old tram that winds its
way up to the summit. You should really make the
effort to reach the top early in the morning when
misty clouds, backlit by the rising sun, sometimes
fill the bay, with just the tops of the islands
peeking above them. It's also well worth visiting
at sunset, when the sun sinks into the hills behind
Rio and the city lights up.

Similarly, the view of both Rio and Corcovado
from Sugar Loaf Mountain is worth seeing at

both ends of the day, when the city assumes quite different appearances.

If you want to see the actual sunrise you will have to take a taxi to San Cristobel Point, which lies outside the park. Although not as high as Corcovado, it still enjoys a commanding view over the bay.

From the top of Sugar Loaf Mountain, it is possible to take a very short helicopter ride that flies you up and around the statue of Christ the Redeemer.

Below: *View from Corcovado Mountain to Sugar Loaf Mountain at dusk*

Rio de Janeiro · Brazil

Rio, however, is about so much more than sights or even natural beauty. No other city in the world epitomizes the 'Life's a Beach' philosophy more than Rio. And where better to see this than at Copacabana and Ipanema? Both immortalized in song, these beaches mirror the character of the cariocas, as the citizens of Rio call themselves. As the clubbers who congregate there to wind down after an all-night party give way to the first of the morning's joggers, the next 24 hours will see everything from holidaymakers to beach boys, from volleyball players to bodybuilders – all set to a background of bossa nova music and perhaps accompanied by a cocktail.

Rio has endured a bad reputation for street crime over the years, but has gone a long way to clean up this problem. As with most major cities, drugs and poverty make certain parts of the city riskier than others, but if you stick to the main areas (which include all the principal tourist sites) and don't carry

valuables conspicuously, you will probably find Rio far less threatening than many European capitals. In fact, the biggest annoyance I suffered – though totally well meaning – was that the locals constantly warned me to be careful with my possessions.

Opposite: *Looking down from Corcovado Mountain*
Below right: *Ipanema Beach*
Below: *Christ the Redeemer*

Rio de Janeiro · Brazil

112

Many airlines fly to Rio from all over the world. Most of the hotels are out along the beaches of Copacabana and Ipanema. The most famous hotel is the Copacabana Palace, run by the Orient Express Group. Even if you do not stay there you should visit the terrace bar for a sundowner. When on the beach, leave all your valuables in your hotel or with the guards posted on the beach by most of the top hotels. The downtown area is quite a way from the beaches, but taxis are cheap and plentiful. The stunning views from Sugar Loaf Mountain and Corcovado are not to be missed.

Opposite above: *Copacabana Beach*
Opposite below: *Santa Teresa tram*
Above: *View from Corcovado Mountain*

Rio de Janeiro · Brazil

18

TAMAN NEGARA RAINFOREST

Malaysia

Dating back over 130 million years, Taman Negara is the oldest rainforest in the world. Home to elephants, the Sumatran rhinoceros and even tigers, as well as 14,000 species of plants and 300 species of birds, the forest is just three hours' drive from the city of Kuala Lumpur, the capital of Malaysia.

The best way to reach the national park that surrounds the forest is to take a bus to Kuala Tembeling, from where you can catch a boat down the river to the park gate at Kuala Tahan. This boat journey is a major part of the Taman Negara experience, and makes you realize just how isolated it is from the outside world. Skirting the border of the park, the trip offers breathtaking views of the forest overhanging the water.

At Kuala Tahan is the Taman Negara Resort, which offers all sorts of accommodation, from cheap hostel beds to luxurious suites. Moored along the river bank opposite are several floating restaurants selling cheap local food. The resort is inside the park and the rainforest starts where the resort stops, although monkeys and birds are no respecters of this and can be seen all over the grounds.

Above: *View from Bukit Teresek*
Opposite: *View from Bukit Teresek with the Sungai Tahan River in the foreground*

Taman Negara Rainforest · Malaysia

Take just a few steps into the rainforest and it closes around you, cutting off the outside world. The trees muffle external noise, obscure the horizon and even change the weather, masking out the sun in a way that can be both sheltering and oppressive. It takes a while to get used to the sound of the rainforest. The continual white noise of insects is punctuated by the shrill shrieks of animals or birds. At night this sound magnifies, and its intensity can sometimes prevent sleep.

With elephants, tigers and poisonous snakes roaming around, and biting insects filling the air, the rainforest can be a hostile environment. Watch out too for the leeches that appear after the regular downpours of rain, littering the paths and ready to latch on to any animal or human that happens to brush past. For many visitors, walking through the rainforest can arouse primeval fears and bring a state of awareness that has been long since lost in normal daily life.

Visitors to the rainforest divide into two types: those sensitive to the majesty, fecundity and minute beauty surrounding them, and those who quite literally can't see the wood for the trees. There are, of course, 'sights' at Taman Negara, such as the waterfall at Lata Berkoh and the hill-top view out over the trees from Bukit Teresek, but the real marvels are all around you: lianas hanging from soaring trees, giant buttress roots that you could hide half a dozen people behind, flashes of colour from darting birds, patterns of dappled light and slow-moving rivers littered with dead vegetation.

A short walk from Kuala Tahan is the longest canopy walkway in the world. Not for the faint-hearted, it leads 430 metres from giant tree to giant

Opposite: *Looking down from the canopy walkway at Kuala Tahan*
Above: *Cascade of Lata Berkoh on the Sungai Tahan River*
Right: *Buttress roots*

tree, sometimes over 50 metres in the air, giving you a bird's-eye view of the plants, and sometimes the wildlife, of the canopy. As the biggest tourist attraction at Taman Negara, the canopy walkway can get very crowded. Most days it is open from 10 a.m. to 3 p.m., but on Friday (the Muslim holy day) it opens at 8 a.m. and shuts at lunchtime. An early start will give you the canopy to yourself for up to an hour, and a much better chance of seeing bird or animal life on the walkway itself.

The resort is quite big, and is best avoided at weekends when it fills up with visitors from the capital. That said, most people don't stray far from the resort, which means that you can still find all the isolation you want by following one of the many trails into the rainforest. You can either hike out and back in a day or stay at one of a network of very basic wildlife hides positioned at watering holes or salt licks. Spending at least one night in a forest hide is an experience. Amid the cacophony of insect noise you wait in both hope and fear of seeing some wildlife, and learn a new appreciation of the environment you are in and the one you have left behind. More intrepid visitors can take a seven-day trek to climb Gunung Tahan volcano, the tallest mountain on the Malaysian peninsula, although it is necessary to organize a guide for this.

Taman Negara rainforest is just three hours by car from Kuala Lumpur. You travel the last stretch by boat and enter the forest by the gate at Kuala Tahan. The Taman Negara Resort has a range of accommodation, but is best avoided at weekends when it can get crowded. The extraordinary sights and sounds are best appreciated from the canopy walkway. Take a trek or spend a night in a forest hide to get the best chance of spotting some of the more elusive wildlife.

Opposite left: *Looking up towards the canopy*
Above: *Trees silhouetted at sunset*

Taman Negara Rainforest · Malaysia

19

JAISALMER FORT
India

Jaisalmer Fort sits in the Thar Desert in the westernmost part of Rajasthan. Located on a former trade route used to transport spices and silks between Arabia and India, Jaisalmer, more than anywhere else in India, appears to have stepped out of the Tales of the Arabian Nights – a collection of ancient folk tales. This is partly due to its location in a remote and inhospitable desert, and partly because of its appearance. Made rich from trade, its merchants built havelis, or merchants' houses, with finely detailed windows and balconies that owe more to Arab style than Indian.

There are bigger and more impressive forts in Rajasthan – such as that at Jodhpur – but few have such an isolated and atmospheric location. Jaisalmer is also reputed to be the only inhabited fort in the world. The maze of tiny streets still rings with daily life, and visitors will often have to push past sacred cows which, unsurprisingly after generations of veneration, act as if they own the place.

The fort, built when the city was founded in 1156, is made up of 99 bastions (projections) linked by battlements that are two walls thick in places. It has seen action a number of times in its

Opposite: *Gadi Sagar tank flooded after the monsoon*
Above: *Detail of balcony carvings*
Right: *The fort at dusk*

Jaisalmer Fort · India

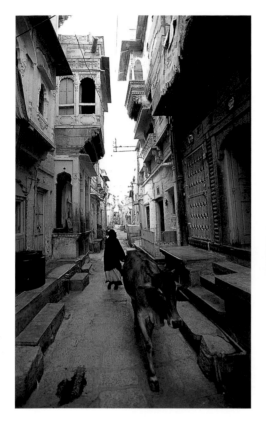

history, and stone missiles — intended to be hurled down on besieging armies — still sit on top of the battlements. Various city states seemed always to be at war, but the fort was first sacked by Muslim invaders in 1294. Rajput warriors would never surrender, preferring to ride out to their inevitable death in battle — an act of mass suicide known as *johar* — while their women and children threw themselves on to fires to preserve their honour.

Although the main attraction of Jaisalmer is the fort itself, there are several things you should aim to see before leaving. Taking up two sides of the main square of the fort, the Rajmahal (city palace) of the former maharaja is seven storeys high and from the top you can look out over the town below and far out into the desert.

There is also a group of exquisitely carved Jain temples, some dating back to the 12th century when the fort was built. Within those it is possible to enter there is a subtle play of light and shade on the carvings, making them even more impressive than those on the outside.

Built almost 700 years ago, the Gadi Sagar tank used to be the sole source of water for the town. Now often completely dry, it sometimes fills during the monsoon season (around September), and you might be rewarded with the rare sight of the fort seemingly perched above a vast lake.

Opposite: *Havelis in Jaisalmer town*
Above left: *Sacred cow in the narrow streets of the fort*
Above right: *Elephant statue outside Nathmal ki Haveli*

Although it has endured for nearly 900 years Jaisalmer Fort is currently in danger of collapse. The city authorities blame this on soil shrinkage arising from the excessive use of water by the guest houses in the fort. Hoteliers deny this claim and blame the city authorities for using drainage pipes that are too small for the job. Whatever the cause, there are moves afoot to ban all business from the fort, with authorities encouraging tourists to stay in the town outside and pay to visit the fort for sightseeing. Whether or not you agree with this strategy, it will certainly change the atmosphere of the place for ever.

Although the camel trains have long gone Jaisalmer remains a trading town, and people come to its market from the villages nearby. Camels, however, still contribute to the town's prosperity as a number of tourist operators offer camel safaris into the surrounding desert.

On the outskirts of the town are the Barra Bagh chatris (royal cenotaphs). These have commanding views over to the fort and offer good vantage points from which to watch the sun set, its last rays turning the town and the fort from the uniform yellow of daytime to a glowing golden hue.

Right: *Detail of carvings in a Jain temple*
Opposite: *Jain temples, inside the fort*

During the peak tourist season (November to January) you can fly to Jaisalmer direct from New Delhi. Outside of these times the airport is closed and you will have to take a night train or a bus from Jodhpur. (There are at least three flights a day from Delhi to Jodhpur.) There are two Heritage hotels in Jaisalmer, the Jawahar Niwas and the Narayan Niwas Palace. The latter has phenomenal views of the fort from its roof. If you fancy a camel safari, you should book with Mr Desert – the face of Jaisalmer.

Jaisalmer Fort · India

125

20

GALAPAGOS ISLANDS

Ecuador

It was on the Galapagos Islands, off the coast of Ecuador, that the process of evolution was first understood. Charles Darwin (1809–82) arrived at the Galapagos in 1835 and stayed for just five weeks, observing and collecting specimens of fauna and flora.

The diversity of life forms he encountered in this small area, and the adaptations they had made to local conditions, led him to formulate his theory of evolution. This was eventually published as *On the Origin of Species by Means of Natural Selection* in 1859, and remains one of the most influential books ever written.

As there are no natural predators on the islands it is still possible to see the diversity of wildlife that so inspired Darwin. Human interference has also been minimal, so the animals and birds seem quite unconcerned by the presence of visitors.

Each species has evolved to exploit the character of individual islands. The blue-footed booby on North Seymour Island, for example, feeds close to the shore, whereas the red-footed booby on more outlying islands, such as Genovesa, feeds a long way out to sea. These

Right: *Nesting pair of blue-footed boobies, North Seymour Island*

Opposite above: *Isla Lobos at sunset*

Opposite below: *Marine iguanas, Bartolome Island*

Galapagos Islands · Ecuador

two birds are fine examples of related species adapting separately to their environments.

The 'signature' animal of the Galapagos for most people is the giant tortoise, which can be seen lumbering around the highlands of Santa Cruz, the second-largest island in the archipelago. Some of these creatures are so old that they might have been seen in their youth by Darwin himself.

Your time in the Galapagos will be remembered as a series of unique wildlife vignettes: snorkelling with sea lions that swim and play within inches of you, and continue leaping in and out of the water long after you have tired and headed for dry land; seeing dozens of sea iguanas clinging haphazardly to a rock; watching from just a few feet away the elaborate courtship ritual of the blue-footed booby; feeling small sharks touch your feet as you wade ashore; noticing a sea turtle cruising majestically along the edge of a coral reef; and, most magically, seeing a humpback whale and her calf surface with a great gout of exhaled air.

The archipelago, which consists of 12 main islands and several smaller ones, is difficult to visit independently. The most practical way to get around is on a cruise of four, seven or even more days. The contrasts between the islands make them very special.

Cruising between them, just as Darwin did nearly 200 years ago, you will feel as though you are getting a privileged insight into an untouched world. At night you will sleep on board the cruise ship, leaving the wildlife in sole occupation of the islands, which are as unspoilt now as they have been since the beginning of time.

Opposite: *Pinnacle Rock, Bartolome Island*
Below: *Sea lions playing, Isla Lobos*

Galapagos Islands · Ecuador

The only practical way to get around the Galapagos Islands is on a short cruise. Metropolitan Touring run a variety of trips but the most popular last from four to seven days. Tame Airlines flies to the islands from Quito, the capital of Ecuador, via Guayaquil, the country's largest city. Be sure to check that your tour operator's fee includes the US $100 park fee (your ticket will be stamped if it does) – if not, you will not be allowed to leave the airport until you pay in cash. Access to the islands by boats and tourists is strictly controlled by the government of Ecuador to minimize the environmental impact of tourism. You cannot wander freely on the islands and the planning of activities and timing is quite rigid. Despite these controls, each day is spectacular. The busiest times are Christmas, Easter and August.

Opposite: *Young great frigate, Genovesa Island*
Above left: *Sally Lightfoot crab*
Above right: *Giant tortoise, Santa Cruz Island*
Below left: *Marine iguanas, James Island*
Below right: *Sea lion, North Seymour Island*

Galapagos Islands · Ecuador

21

MANHATTAN ISLAND
New York, USA

From the imposing figure of the Statue of Liberty to the flashing neon signs of Times Square, from the green oasis that is Central Park to the canyon-like streets full of yellow cabs, everything about New York seems familiar, even if you have never been there before. Like no other city, it has entered into our collective consciousness through a lifetime of images, yet no superlative can really do justice to its aggressive boldness.

Of course it would be churlish not to mention another image of Manhattan burnt into the world's memory: the sight of crashing planes and burning, tumbling buildings irrevocably affected more than just the skyline of a city.

Sitting at the mouth of the Hudson River, New York is divided into five boroughs, and Manhattan is the one that forms the heart of the city. Actually an island, Manhattan is much smaller than the first-time visitor might imagine, and can be circled in just two to three hours on the famous Circle Line boat trip. Its isolation and compactness have given Manhattan a self-sufficiency and character quite distinct from the rest of the city. Its people, too, are just as they appear in the movies –

Above: *Brooklyn Bridge at sunset*
Opposite: *The Statue of Liberty at sunset*

a cosmopolitan melting pot of larger-than-life characters, treating each other and visitors with sometimes alarming frankness. Each borough of New York is made up of neighbourhoods, often where various immigrant communities have congregated over the years and coloured the city with the particular feel of their homeland. Chinatown and Little Italy, for example, feel like opposite ends of the world, but in Manhattan they are separated by just the width of a street.

Navigating the city's grid is relatively easy and the subway is simple to use – keep a subway map handy. Streets run east–west, avenues run north–south and the length of a block between two streets is usually much shorter than that between two avenues.

Ironically, Manhattan's high-rise landscape is best seen from above to really appreciate the block after block of skyscrapers that all but fill the island. The famous viewing platform on the 86th floor of the Empire State Building offers undoubtedly the best views of the whole city.

New York throbs with energy – commercially, socially and culturally. Not for nothing is it described as the 'city that never sleeps'. From the moment you arrive, whether by air, sea or road, you will feel that energy and be infused with it until you must reluctantly tear yourself away.

Six per cent of Manhattan is taken up by Central Park, which is a haven from the traffic noise and commotion although it's in the heart of the city. From its south-east corner you get a great view of the park against a backdrop of characteristic New York buildings on bustling Fifth Avenue – just one more contrast in this city of extremes.

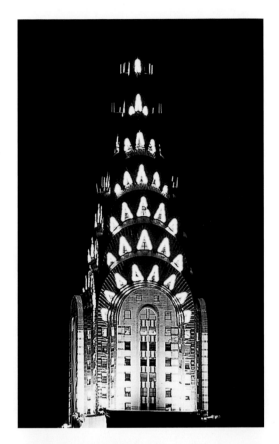

Opposite above: *Times Square*
Opposite below: *Midtown cityscape*
Above: *The Chrysler Building*
Right: *Wall Street, with the New York Stock Exchange in the background*

Manhattan Island · New York, USA

There is a wide range of hotel accommodation in Manhattan and you should work out which area you fancy staying in and then pick a hotel. Getting around Manhattan is easy. The subway is inexpensive, although the maps take some getting used to. Taxis are cheap and plentiful, and part of the whole experience. Tipping has reached near-epidemic proportions in New York, and you should expect to add at least 15% to restaurant and bar bills, and taxi fares.

Left: *The Empire State Building (left) and the Chrysler Building from the Hudson River*

Below: *View across the pond to Central Park South and Fifth Avenue*

Opposite: *Chase Manhattan Plaza (the building at the lower left) and surrounding buildings*

Manhattan Island · New York, USA

22

LAKE TITICACA
Bolivia and Peru

Lake Titicaca has a haunting and desolate beauty. The intensity of the rich, dark blue of the water is unique among freshwater lakes and makes the wide expanses of sky and landscape look even more stark and exceptional. At more than 3800 metres above sea level, Lake Titicaca is the highest navigable lake in the world. The clarity of the air at this altitude, combined with the hues of the lake and its islands, produces a colour palette of intense vibrancy.

The lake, which is 176 km long and some 50 km wide, and straddles Bolivia and Peru, is considered to be sacred by many of the local people, who believe that spirits live in its deep waters. In Andean creation myths Lake Titicaca was the birthplace of civilization, and the sun, moon and stars rose out of it.

   To really appreciate the lake and the people who live on it, you have to go out on to one of the islands, where the scenery and culture are totally different from those of the mainland. Many tourists head straight for the floating islands of Uros, which are created from bundles of floating reeds. As the lower reeds rot and fall away new ones are added to the top to maintain the

Right: View of the Bolivian Cordillera from Isla de la Luna (Island of the Moon)

structure, a method of construction that dates back to antiquity.

The islands of Amantani and Taquile, which are some three hours by boat from the town of Puno, are less affected by tourism. The people on these islands speak Quechua, the oldest living language in Peru, and their traditions survive largely unscathed by the 21st century. The people of Taquile still wear clothing that they weave from the wool of alpacas. The women wear layered skirts and shawls, whereas the men adorn themselves with embroidered waistbands and woollen caps.

Lake Titicaca · Bolivia and Peru

Amantani, the larger of the two islands, is inhabited by about 800 families – fishermen, farmers and weavers. Ancient stone walls divide terraces that belong to different families. There are two peaks on the island; one topped by the ruins of the Temple of Pachamama and the other by the ruins of the Temple of Pachatata. These pre-Incan structures represent Mother Earth and Father Earth respectively. Every January the Fiesta de la Santa Tierra (Festival of the Sacred Land) splits the island, with half the people attending each of the ruined temples.

Opposite: *Boats on the island of Taquile with the island of Amantani in the background*

Left: *Drop-spinning wool thread to make traditional clothing on Taquile*

Below: *Inca ruins on Isla del Sol (Island of the Sun)*

Lake Titicaca · Bolivia and Peru

The high altitude makes the hike up to Pachamama strenuous, but the views across to the mountains of the Cordillera Real on the Bolivian side of the lake make it all worthwhile. The hill is also a perfect place to watch the sunset when the colours of the lake and the sky become even more vibrant and intense.

The snow-capped Cordillera Real is visible from most of the lake and forms a distinct border between the stark expanses of water and sky. Sometimes the vista is softened by a flock of flamingos strutting imperiously across the shallows of the lake. This incongruous smattering of pink brings some relief from the unyielding colours of Lake Titicaca.

Left: *Island of Amantani, with the Bolivian Cordillera in the background*

Puno is the gateway city on the Peruvian side of Lake Titicaca. The train journey from Cuzco to Puno takes a day and passes through some beautiful high-altitude terrain. The town of Copacabana in Bolivia, on the southern half of the lake, can be reached from La Paz. The famous views of the snow-covered Bolivian Cordillera are best seen from the islands accessible from Copacabana: Isla del Sol and Isla de la Luna. Do not underestimate the effects of the altitude here, especially if you are planning strenuous activities such as hiking on the islands. The ferry that crosses the lake between Peru and Bolivia takes just 12 hours.

Lake Titicaca · Bolivia and Peru

23

MONET'S GARDEN
Giverny, France

For anyone with even a passing knowledge of the work of Claude Monet (1840–1926), his gardens at Giverny in Normandy, France, will be instantly familiar. The tranquil pond of water lilies inspired some of the greatest paintings of the 19th century.

Monet first saw Giverny from a train window. He moved there in 1883 and started to create the gardens, which he came to regard as his greatest achievement. They are places of light and shadow, where subtle reflections of foliage and flowers in the cool green waters are fleetingly transformed by the fluctuating light of the changeable Normandy weather.

The gardens, intersected by many small gravel paths, slope gently down to the lily pond, which is surprisingly small but very atmospheric. A path skirts their perimeter, offering a range of views and variations in light as you walk along it. Some of the views are open, others punctuated by weeping willows.

Monet's house at Giverny is large and rustic, and visitors can walk around it and look out on to

Above: *Monet's house*
Opposite: *The bridge at the eastern end of the water-lily pond*

the views that inspired him so much. He watched the colours gradually change as the seasons passed and woke up each morning to look at them from his bedroom window.

The largest of the garden paths – the Grande Allée – leads from the house to the Japanese bridge, well known from Monet's numerous depictions of it. The gardens are now divided by a road, but both parts are connected by a tunnel.

Since his earliest days as a painter, Monet worked in the open air rather than a studio. He believed in trying to 'capture the moment' in his paintings, which meant that he had to work fast. This technique created an impression

of the subject matter, rather than a detailed description, and led to its exponents being called 'Impressionists'.

During his time at Giverny Monet was often visited by his artistic contemporaries, including Cézanne, Renoir, Matisse and Pissarro, few of whom enjoyed recognition during their lifetimes. It is now staggering to imagine so much talent gathered in one small place. Monet died at Giverny in 1926 at the age of 86.

Above left: *A painter at the water-lily pond*
Above right: *The water-lily pond*

Monet's gardens in the village of Giverny are 65 km north-west of Paris, off the
A13 motorway. The nearest English Channel ferry ports are Le Havre and Dieppe. Vernon,
8 km from the A13 and 5 km from Giverny, is the nearest useful town and has good
accommodation and restaurants. The gardens get extremely crowded in the middle of the
day, so aim to arrive as early as possible. They are open daily except Mondays (to allow
select artists to paint) from 9.30 a.m. to 6 p.m. from 1 April to 1 November. The most popular
months to visit are July and August, when the water lilies flower. Accommodation in Giverny
itself is limited. A website (www.giverny.org) has information about where to stay, transport
and flowering times.

Above: *Monet's bedroom*
Opposite: *Poppy seed heads*

24

NGORONGORO CRATER

Tanzania

The Ngorongoro Crater feels so cut off from the outside world that you almost expect to see long-extinct dinosaurs, not just teeming wildlife, roaming within its steep, forbidding walls. Veined by the forces that created them, these walls rise 600 metres above the flat floor.

Ngorongoro is actually a caldera, not a crater, formed when a volcano collapsed millions of years ago. At more than 20 km across, it is the largest complete, unflooded caldera in the world. As you look down from the rim you could be forgiven for thinking that Ngorongoro is completely deserted and rumours of its bounty exaggerated. But closer inspection through binoculars reveals signs of life. Those ant-like dots moving slowly across the caldera floor are actually bristling Cape buffalo, arguably the most dangerous animal in Africa. Only then does the true scale of the caldera become apparent.

Ngorongoro is so large that it has its own distinct weather patterns. Mist and cloud often coat the densely forested flanks of the caldera, sometimes spilling over the edge. Occasionally,

Above: *Common zebra*
Opposite: *Looking down into the caldera*

Ngorongoro Crater · Tanzania

these clouds are so dense that they fill the bowl of the caldera. Leaving the comfort of your lodge and journeying down to the caldera floor in these conditions can become something of a leap of faith. The weather can be quite localized. It can be cloudy, even raining, on one side while the other side is bathed in bright sunshine.

For all the beauty and majesty of Ngorongoro, it is the wildlife that is the greatest draw. The walls act as both refuge and restraint, trapping and protecting a surprising amount of big game. The caldera is home to some 30 black rhino – the largest concentration of the species left on the continent. In the dry season they can be remarkably difficult to spot, as they spend much of the day asleep in the long grass; but when the grass is short and green they virtually litter the caldera floor, bringing back memories of a bygone age when they used to stomp and snort their bad-tempered way across the whole of Africa.

Ngorongoro is also famous for its lion population, much filmed for television documentaries, but apparently chronically inbred. The isolation of the caldera prevents fresh blood from wandering in from the nearby Serengeti.

In the middle of the caldera lies Lake Magadi, a vast soda lake frequented by flamingos. The population fluctuates from a few thousand to literally hundreds of thousands in June, when the flamingos flock back from their migration to the Great Rift Valley.

Most common African wildlife is found in the caldera, with the notable exception of giraffe which find the walls too steep. Most of the animals are permanent residents, although elephants and buffalo are often to be found feeding on the upper rim, especially at night.

Opposite above: *Clouds rearing up over the walls of the caldera*
Opposite below: *Wildebeest on the caldera floor*
Above: *Female ostrich on the caldera floor*

The caldera officially opens just after dawn. The tracks on the north rim are vertiginous, requiring a four-wheel-drive vehicle. The track on the south rim, servicing the Sopa Lodge, is much less steep, allowing quicker and safer access to the caldera floor.

Don't be surprised if you see Masai *morani* (warriors) bringing cattle down into the caldera. Although the Masai often come here to make money by posing for tourist photographs, they also have grazing and watering rights for their cattle. If you wonder at the wisdom of bringing a potential food source into lion territory, you will be told that after generations of experience the lions have a healthy fear of the Masai, and tend to disappear as soon as they arrive – much to the chagrin of the safari guides.

Below: *Looking down from the caldera rim*
Opposite: *Elephants on the caldera floor*

The Ngorongoro Crater is about six hours' drive from Arusha in northern Tanzania. You can fly to Arusha from Dar es Salaam or Zanzibar with Air Excel. Accommodation can be found in lodges overlooking the caldera. Most are on the relatively crowded north side but Sopa Lodge, which offers fine views of the sunset and uses the much safer access road, stands in splendid isolation on the south side. Safari guides can be hired from Abercrombie & Kent, the oldest established travel company in Africa. For the full safari experience you could combine Ngorongoro with the nearby Lake Manyara National Park, or even the world-famous Serengeti National Park.

Ngorongoro Crater · Tanzania

25

SANTORINI
Greece

*Sitting in the peaceful town of Oia on the island of Santorini
(known as Thira to the Greeks), watching the sun slip
quietly into the sea, it is hard to imagine the colossal forces
of nature that blew the island apart around 1550 BC.*

This volcanic eruption is believed to have devastated an outpost of the advanced Minoan civilization, which had been established on the island before 2000 BC, leading to many theories that Santorini is in fact Plato's lost city of Atlantis.

The present-day island of Santorini is formed from the circular caldera of the volcano. The circle is incomplete in places and, flooded by the sea, forms a natural harbour so vast that visiting ferries and cruise ships are dwarfed by it.

A small island in the middle of the caldera is actually the centre of the volcano and can be reached by boat. You can even walk around its rocky 'moonscape' and stand next to the still-steaming mouth of the volcano that created Santorini in the first place. Like most smoking volcanoes, it seems to hold the threat of erupting at any time. (The last eruption happened in the 1920s and an earthquake devastated the island in 1956.)

The jagged walls of the caldera rise up to 300 metres above the sea. The highest cliffs are at Fira, the capital of Santorini, and the adjacent town of Firostefani, now all but swallowed up by

Right: *Church bell, Fira*
Opposite: *Traditional blue-domed church, Oia*

Fira. These towns are built on the very rim of the caldera, overlooking the waters far below.

Each town has its own harbour at the foot of the cliffs, reachable by a zigzag path from the top. Fira now has a modern cable car, and it is only the tourists from cruise ships and ferries who make the long hike up. If you can't face walking, you can rent a donkey from one of the irascible old men who spend the day leading their mounts up and down the path. Come sunset, the donkeys leave Fira at a gallop, glad to be on their way home, and you have to take care not to be knocked over in the rush.

Santorini is renowned for its white-walled, blue-domed churches, which are often photographed against the dark blue waters of the Aegean. In fact, there are so many churches on this island that you have to wonder who on earth goes to them. Is there some feud that prevents all the islanders attending the same one?

Many of the churches are still in use, and you will often see grey-bearded priests, dressed entirely in black, hurrying from church to church, presumably trying to find their flock in one of the numerous possible locations.

Like so many other places Santorini has been comprehensively taken over by the tourist trade, and most of the fishermen's cottages have now been converted into hotels, restaurants or guest houses. Despite this, however, the island still retains much of its original character. Oia, especially, still has a sprinkling of locals living among all the tourist places, and outside some of the cottages, hung with baskets of brightly coloured flowers, fishing nets await repair and scraggy cats doze in tiny front yards.

Opposite above: *Blue-domed church, Oia*
Opposite below: *Town of Fira perched on top of soaring cliffs*
Above: *Small chapel, Firostefani*

Santorini · Greece

160

Santorini is easily reached by ferry,
or internal flight on Olympic Airways,
from Athens. There are even some direct
flights from European airports during
the summer season. Accommodation
can be hard to find during the summer
months, so it is advisable to book in
advance. One of the best hotels in Fira
is the Santorini Palace, which overlooks
the caldera. The bus service around the
island is fairly limited but there are taxis
and car hire is quite easy. Most of the
beaches are outside the main towns
and, although the sand is volcanic
black, they are ideal spots to while
away the day.

Left: *Traditional houses in Oia*
Above: *Cross on top of a church, Fira*

26

THE AMPHITHEATRE
Drakensberg, South Africa

Stand by the edge of the 850-metre cliffs of the amphitheatre of the uKhahlamba-Drakensberg Park and you will be dwarfed. The cliffs are a massive horseshoe of rock, often filled with swirling clouds that appear to change their mood as you watch. Sometimes they fill the basin, making the view of a few seconds ago seem like a mirage. At other times they just disappear, revealing the valley below.

The cliffs of the amphitheatre drop vertically down to a green valley and offer commanding views of the Devil's Tooth rock formation. Part of the way along the upper rim of the amphitheatre the 'bridal veil' Tugela Falls spills 850 metres over the edge to form the source of the Tugela River.

Drakensberg is Afrikaans for 'dragon mountain' and uKhahlamba is Zulu for 'barrier of spears' – fitting names for the 320-km escarpment of harsh and jutting rock that forms the border between Lesotho and the Republic of South Africa.

At the top of the escarpment is a tableland plateau. In Lesotho, the 'Kingdom of the Sky', this is a unique and fragile habitat for wildlife and many rare plant species. In the beautiful alpine

Above: *Sunrise near Cathedral Peak*
Opposite: *Hills in the Giant's Castle area*

landscape of mountain streams and lush grasses are small wild flowers that have adapted to the climate, which can turn from fine and bright to cold and stormy in minutes. In fact, the plateau's great height means that the temperature there can be freezing while the parklands at the bottom can be warm and sunny.

The best way to reach the plateau is to drive to the Golden Gate Highlands National Park (a park within the Drakensberg area). From here there are two ways to reach the top of the escarpment: a two- to three-hour hike up a steep trail, or a climb up a notorious chain ladder. Whichever route you choose, it is wise to make a very early start as mists often sweep in during the late morning and can completely obscure the view.

Tucked away in numerous caves around the Drakensberg are some of the finest examples of rock art in Africa. In the Drakensberg area alone there are hundreds of sites with thousands of rock paintings. They were painted by the San people who used to roam over much of southern Africa but are now confined to a few pockets around the Kalahari Desert in Botswana. Diminutive in stature, they are often (erroneously) known as the Bushmen of the Kalahari. Their rock paintings, which are usually found in shelters or overhangs, record the life and history of the San people but, more importantly, are thought to have a spiritual significance as openings to the spirit world. The oldest paintings are about 25,000 years old

The Amphitheatre · Drakensberg, South Africa

and the most recent may be just 200 years old. Pigments were ground from iron oxides for the reds and yellows, manganese oxide or burnt bone for black and fine clay for white. The artists often painted over earlier images or added to existing ones.

A variety of terrains in the park are worth exploring, and you could also visit the Cathedral Peak and the Giant's Castle, the latter involving a five-day trek along the escarpment, or a day's drive.

Opposite: *View of Devil's Tooth from Golden Gate Highlands National Park*
Above: *Hills in the Giant's Castle area dappled with shadow*
Right: *San rock art at Main Caves, Giant's Castle*

The Amphitheatre · Drakensberg, South Africa

The Amphitheatre · Drakensberg, South Africa

The Drakensberg escarpment is about two hours' drive from Pietermaritzburg and a scenic five hours' drive from Johannesburg. The various locations and lodges along the escarpment are relatively close to one another as the crow flies but you should use the main roads. Do not be tempted to use more direct routes as these are rougher, carry very little traffic and have no services. The parks are administered by KwaZulu-Natal Wildlife, which runs a number of lodges and camps that make access to the various sections of the park easy. Getting to the top of the uKhahlamba escarpment involves an arduous hike from the Golden Gate Highlands National Park. You should make a very early start to avoid the late morning mists that often obscure the views.

Opposite: *View of Devil's Tooth from Golden Gate Highlands National Park*
Above: *View below Giant's Castle; the Giant's Castle*
formation is in the background, towards the left

The Amphitheatre · Drakensberg, South Africa

27

ZANZIBAR

Tanzania

Zanzibar. Even the name is exotic, conjuring up
images of sultans and explorers and of wooden
Arab dhows redolent with the aroma of spices.

Arriving by boat from Dar es Salaam, you will see the waterfront of Zanzibar town looking much as it did in the days when Victorian explorers used the island as a staging post for their expeditions into the interior of Africa. (David Livingstone, who discovered the Victoria Falls, started out from

here, as did Henry Morton Stanley, the journalist dispatched to find him.)

Right in the middle of the waterfront is the Sultan's Palace. Built in the 19th century, it was called the House of Wonders because it had electricity and the first lift in East Africa. After

years of neglect, it has now been restored and houses a fine museum.

Zanzibar has a colourful history. Omani sultans ruled much of the Swahili coast from the island, establishing the trade routes that still lead from here to the Middle East. Their domain dwindled in the days of the British Empire, and finally ceased with the bloody revolution of 1956.

The long history of Zanzibar has its darker side. During the 18th and 19th centuries it was the main base for the trade in African slaves brought from the interior by Arab traders, who often purchased their captives from warring tribes. The slaves were sold to European and American merchants, and shipped in appalling conditions to the Americas and the Caribbean.

Right: *Traditional Arab dhow*
Below: *Waterfront at Zanzibar town showing the House of Wonders*

Zanzibar · Tanzania

It is still possible to visit the old slave pens, but an Anglican cathedral has been built on the site of the slave market. The altar is on the very spot where the whipping post once stood, and the cross beside it is made from the tree under which Livingstone died. During his time as a missionary Livingstone became a tireless crusader for the abolition of slavery, but the trade continued illegally for some years after it was banned.

The heart of Zanzibar town, built of stone, is a tangle of narrow winding streets that seem to lead everywhere and nowhere. Look out for the ornate, carved wooden doors, many of which date from the time of the sultans. They were designed both to display and to protect the wealth of the house-owners.

In the early morning, when the tourist shops are closed, life in the town seems to continue much as it has for hundreds of years. It is not difficult to imagine explorers combing its streets, looking for supplies and porters.

Everywhere you go you will be greeted with shouts of *jambo* (hello) and *karibu* (welcome). Take a walk to the old dhow harbour and you can watch fishermen haggling with locals over their catch. You can also get a close-up view of the remarkable sailing boats, held together entirely with wooden pegs, that have been used along the Swahili coast ever since the Arabs first arrived from Oman. Although still used to move goods between East Africa and the Middle East, their use is dying out.

While the town has a number of top-quality restaurants, the nicest place to eat is at the Jamituri Gardens on the waterfront. From sunset every day locals set up open-air stalls to cook and sell some of the freshly caught fish landed every morning. You can get crab and lobster for just a few dollars, and wash it down with a glass of freshly squeezed sugar-cane juice, while chatting with the friendly Zanzibaris about everything from politics to football.

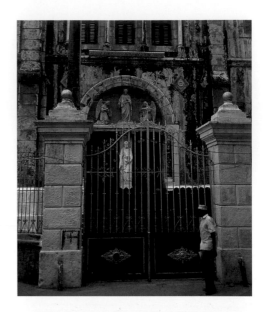

Above, top: *St Joseph's Catholic cathedral, built by the French in 1898*
Above: *Cooked food at Jamituri Gardens*
Opposite above: *Buildings on the waterfront*
Opposite below: *Dhow harbour*

Zanzibar · Tanzania

171

Zanzibar · Tanzania

Zanzibar lies off the coast of Tanzania,
a few hours by ferry boat from Dar es
Salaam. There are a number of morning
departures, returning mid-afternoon.
Details are posted on the ferry dock
but steer clear of touts and buy your
tickets directly from the ticket office.
Alternatively, Air Excel fly from Dar es
Salaam to Zanzibar and sometimes from
Zanzibar to Arusha. Although Dodoma
is the new official capital of Tanzania,
many flights arrive at Dar es Salaam.
There is a wide range of accommodation
in Zanzibar town, the best of which
are the Serena or the Tembo House.
The northern and eastern coasts of
Zanzibar have a number of beautiful
beaches, with accommodation ranging
from simple beach huts to luxurious
resorts. Local travel agents will arrange
reservations and transfers.

Above: *Zanzibari carved wooden door*

28

MAKALU
Himalayas, Nepal

*High in the Himalayas, amid mighty peaks encrusted with glaciers,
is Makalu, the fifth-highest mountain in the world. Although less
well known than other peaks in the region, notably Everest and
the Annapurna range, Makalu has arguably the most stunning
scenery. Set in the remote Makalu Barun National Park, it has the
added advantage of being away the centres of political unrest .*

Like many of the peaks in the Himalayas, Makalu is considered a holy mountain. Its name is said to be derived from the Sanskrit word 'Mahakala', the personification of death and rebirth, which, for Tibetan Buddhists, represents the power of the Lord Buddha's protection. The mountain is believed to be the kingdom of Mahakala.

The Himalayas are built on a massive scale, and there is little to prepare you for their immensity and beauty. But it is not a stationary beauty. Distant avalanches can occasionally be heard, thundering like express trains, and the mountains appear to alter in shape, colour and mood as the light and cloud formations change throughout the day. This is a transfixing sight that you can sit and watch for hours. Sometimes whole sections will be illuminated by the

Above: *View of Everest from the glaciers at the foot of Makalu*
Opposite: *Lake scene on the Makalu trek*

golden afternoon light, casting great shadows into valleys and crevasses. At other times vast swathes of mountains will turn blue or be completely obscured by swirling clouds.

The air is so clear at this height that it is always possible to make out the shape of the snow-capped peaks, and you can almost read by the light of the stars that fill the night sky.

To visit the beautiful and remote Makalu takes both time and effort, as the trek is not easy and takes nine days from the airstrip at Tumlingtar. Much of the trek is done at altitude, which is debilitating until you become acclimatized.

The trek takes you over many passes, through verdant farmland and past many steeply terraced hillsides. *Khambas* (farms) within just a few hours

of the base camp remind you that people actually live in this harsh environment – a humbling thought when you grow weary of the regular downpours that leave the paths littered with leeches. However, along these ancient and well-travelled routes are a number of tea shops and it is easy to meet and talk to the local farmers and porters over a refreshing cup of chai (tea).

From the Makalu region you should be able to see four of the five highest mountains in the world: Everest (8848 metres), Kangchenjunga (8586

Above: *Trail through a farm near the Arun River valley*
Opposite above left: *Makalu peak*
Opposite above right: *Mountain seen from Makalu base camp*
Opposite below: *High mountain lake on the Makalu trek*

Makalu · Himalayas, Nepal

metres), Lhotse (8516 metres) and, of course, Makalu itself (8463 metres). (The world's second-highest peak is K2 on the Pakistan border.)

If you have the energy you could trek to the Everest base camp which lies just west of Makalu. It is also possible to follow the standard Everest trek back to Lukla and then catch a flight back to Kathmandu. Although it follows a much more well-trodden route and doesn't enjoy the quiet solitude of the direct route to Makalu, it does at least avoid trekking back the way you have come.

Opposite: *View from the glaciers at the foot of Makalu*
Above, top: *Makalu peak*
Above: *Glacial ice*

The trek to Makalu starts from the airstrip at Tumlingtar, which can be reached from the Nepalese capital, Kathmandu. From here it is an arduous nine-day trek to the mountain and, of course, nine days back again. Unless you are an experienced trekker you would be wise to organize this with a local trekking company in Kathmandu and take a guide with you. The best times to trek are April and May, and late September through October.

Makalu · Himalayas, Nepal

29

LALIBELA
Ethiopia

Mystery and myth surround the creation of the carved stone churches of Lalibela in the remote highlands of Ethiopia. Some say that the churches were built by crusaders returning from the Holy Land, but Ethiopians believe that they were created with the help of angels by King Lalibela over 1000 years ago.

The most magnificent of the churches is Bet Giorgis, the House of Saint George, named after the patron saint of Ethiopia. Carved out of solid rock in the shape of a cross, the church is a structural marvel. Builders would first have created the 6-metre-deep courtyard to form the 'exterior' of the building, before carving the doors and windows into it, and then hollowing out the rock beyond to make the interior. The immensity of this task, and the precision it required, are almost inconceivable, especially bearing in mind that all the work was done by hand.

In all there are 11 carved churches at Lalibela, including Bet Medhane Alem (the House of Emmanuel) which, at 800 square metres, is the largest carved monolithic structure in the world. Its great bulk is supported by a total of 72 pillars, half of which are inside and half outside.

Above: *Bet Giorgis*
Opposite: *Priest with an ancient bible outside the Asheton Maryam monastery*

Although the churches would be evocative as deserted ruins, they are still in constant use and each has a resident priest who, with a little prompting, will bring out a church treasure to show you. Sometimes this might be an ancient Bible, perhaps 700 years old, handwritten in the ancient religious language of Ge'ez on goatskin pages. More usually, the priest will produce the church cross. In various intricate shapes, some crosses date back to the days of King Lalibela himself.

Pilgrims seem to come to Lalibela from all over Ethiopia, and can often be seen praying in the churches. There are also a number of semi-permanent ascetics, who stay in Lalibela praying and can be seen sitting around the churches reading well-worn bibles.

On 19 January Timkat (Epiphany) is celebrated at Lalibela. This is a tremendously colourful festival when the holy tabots (which are believed to be replicas of the Ark of the Covenant) are taken from each church and paraded through the town.

The official religion of Lalibela is Ethiopian Orthodox, a form of Christianity that the country adopted in the 4th century. This choice was freely made by the people, unlike in the rest of Africa where Christianization was the result of missionary work, centuries later.

Below: *Looking down into the courtyard around Bet Giorgis*
Opposite above: *Painted interior of a church at Lalibela*
Opposite below left: *Bet Giorgis*
Opposite below right: *Pilgrim reading an old bible*

Lalibela · Ethiopia

183

Although synonymous in the West with famine and disaster, Ethiopia is steeped in ancient and biblical history. The Queen of Sheba is believed to have come from here, a native of the northern city of Aksum, at that time the centre of a great and powerful civilization. It was the break-up of the Aksumite Empire that caused King Lalibela to flee south and set up a new capital, where he built his churches.

Many Ethiopians believe that Haile Selassie, Emperor of Ethiopia from 1930 to 1974, could trace his lineage directly to the illegitimate son of King Solomon and the Queen of Sheba. This son was said to have brought the Ark of the Covenant back to Ethiopia, and it is believed to reside in Aksum.

A worthwhile excursion from Lalibela is up to the Asheton Maryam monastery carved into the rock on a desolate, windswept plateau a couple of hours' walk from Lalibela. Here you can see a fascinating collection of paintings and relics, and also observe the harsh conditions in which many local people live.

Above left: *Pilgrim praying outside Bet Medhane Alem (the House of Emmanuel)*
Above right: *Pilgrim at Lalibela*
Opposite: *Priest of Bet Giorgis*

Ethiopian Airlines flies from airports around the world to the Ethiopian capital, Addis Ababa, and offers internal flights to Lalibela. (The alternative is a hard two-day drive.) It is also possible to get a flight pass on the so-called 'historic route' service that takes in Aksum, Bahar Dar, Gonder and Lalibela. Accommodation in Lalibela can be basic. One of the best hotels is the Roha, part of the government-run Ghion chain. Book in advance, especially during the Timkat celebrations. A ticket costing about £39 ($50) will get you into the site and is valid for 5 days. A local guide is useful – especially to translate when you meet the priests. Most hotels can provide guides, but make sure their English is up to the job.

Lalibela · Ethiopia

30

MACHU PICCHU
Peru

Everything about Machu Picchu makes you marvel that it ever came to exist. The lost city of the Incas is built on a saddle-shaped ridge slung between two giant peaks. Near-vertical slopes drop away on either side, down to a massive bend in the Urubamba River. What could have motivated the Incas to undertake such a construction at this remote location in the Andean cordillera?

Machu Picchu, built over 700 years ago and hidden by jungle since the 16th century, was rediscovered in 1911. It consists of about 200 buildings, which include dwellings and temples, a central plaza and a royal palace, all flanked by terraces for farming.

The stone for the buildings was mined from a quarry and shaped using bronze tools, then smoothed with sand in order to fit tightly together. No mortar was used in the construction. Even after many centuries of wear and tear, the precision is amazing; it would be impossible to slide a piece of paper between many of the blocks.

Below: *Ruins seen from the summit of Machu Picchu peak*
Opposite: *Machu Picchu with Huayna Picchu in the background*

Machu Picchu · Peru

188

Machu Picchu is notable for the way that existing rock features were incorporated into the design. Inevitably, the craftsmanship on sacred buildings is the finest.

For spectacular views, make the steep climb up to Wayna Picchu, the mountain behind Machu Picchu. Alternatively, climb to the top of the less crowded Machu Picchu peak, which catches the first rays of the rising sun. Both mountains overlook the entire site, down to the river below, which puts the Incas' great achievement of construction into perspective.

The Incas worshipped the sun god Inti, so the summer solstice was the most important day in their calendar, and the Temple of the Sun their most important building. In fact, all their temples and sacred sites were designed to mark solar and astrological events. A stone, Intihuatana ('Hitching Post of the Sun'), is the focus of a major religious site where a ritual was performed, in the shortening

Left: *Sunrise over Machu Picchu*
Above: *Royal Tomb, a cave under the Temple of the Sun*

days before the winter solstice, to prevent the sun disappearing. Similar stones were at other Inca sites, but were damaged or destroyed by Spanish conquistadores. The one at Machu Picchu survived because the site was never discovered.

The population of Machu Picchu is believed to have numbered over a thousand, and the people were so distant from other settlements that they would have produced much of their own food. This accounts for the intricately terraced fields, which have survived remarkably intact thanks to the care and skill that went into their construction. Maize and potatoes were grown, and advanced irrigation techniques were used to ensure that rainwater didn't just run off down the hill to the Urubamba River far below.

No one knows for sure why Machu Picchu was built. Some surmise that it was a royal or religious retreat for one of the Inca rulers. Certainly its remote location and altitude of nearly 2500 metres would seem to rule out any trade or military function. Whatever its use, the obvious effort that went into its construction indicates that it was considered important and held in high regard by those who created it.

Above: *Dwellings near the Temple of the Sun*
Right: *Terraces below the Intihuatana*
Opposite: *Dwellings on eastern side of the site*

All trips to Machu Picchu begin and end in Cuzco. The train journey from Cuzco to Aguas Calientes, the town in the river valley below the ruins, takes four hours. Buses go to and from the town to the ruins from 6 a.m. until 5.30 p.m. The trains from Cuzco arrive mid-morning and leave late in the afternoon, so the least crowded times at the ruins are the beginning and the end of each day. The fitter and more adventurous can take the three-day Inca Trail to reach Machu Picchu. There is plenty of accommodation in Aguas Calientes. However, the best place to stay for access and proximity to the ruins is the Machu Picchu Sanctuary Lodge, an Orient Express Hotel. It is the only hotel next to the ruins and a stay there is a unique experience.

31

ULURU
Australia

From whatever angle you look at it, Uluru (commonly known as Ayers Rock) dominates the surrounding landscape. Seen from afar, it is the only feature that breaks an otherwise flat horizon, while up close – such as on the approach road from the cultural centre – it looms above you, completely filling your vehicle's windscreen.

Uluru is the largest monolith (single piece of rock) in the world. Composed of sandstone, which is normally grey, it has become red through a process of oxidization (in effect, rusting).

As you get closer to Uluru, its brooding mass yields up a wealth of detail. Follow the walk that skirts the base of the rock and you will see great flutes that spawn torrential waterfalls when it rains, which is quite often despite the parched landscape round about. Elsewhere are caves and crevices eroded into the rock – many of which have been woven into Aboriginal creation tales – and right up close the rock is stippled and textured in a variety of ways.

Anangu (local Aboriginal people) are the Traditional Owners of Uluru, which has great cultural significance to them. Two of the walks on the rock illustrate Aboriginal respect for natural places, and pass by apparently insignificant features in the landscape that they hold deeply sacred.

Right: Uluru at sunset (Uluru-Kata Tjuta National park is a world heritage area)
Opposite: The western side of Uluru

Uluṟu · Australia

193

The Mutitjulu Walk takes you through an area that has been inhabited by Aboriginal people for thousands of years to the Mutitjulu waterhole. Various features along this walk are said to have resulted from a great fight between two ancestral snakes, Kuniya and Liru.

The Mala Walk takes you around some of the places used by the Mala (hare-wallaby) people for a religious ceremony (Inma), which involved their menfolk climbing to the top of Uluru. At one time, following a route to the top was a 'must' for tourists. Though many still do, this is now discouraged because it causes offence to Anangu. While no one actually prevents you from climbing, Anangu request that you don't do it.

Balancing the needs of Anangu and the tourists shows the difficulties of resolving the differences between a culture that pretty much values and reveres everything with a culture that seems to revere almost nothing.

Some 45 km away from Uluru lie the domed peaks of Kata Tjuta (the Olgas). Some of these are even taller than Uluru and are also held sacred by Anangu. Like Uluru, the peaks are spectacular at sunrise and sunset, and you should aim to spend at least a day exploring them and walking the sacred Valley of the Winds.

The images in this book have all been taken under the strict rules governing commercial photography in the Uluru-Kata Tjuta National Park, which are intended to prevent pictures of sacred sites being published and offending Anangu. This does, however, effectively rule out photographing almost half the site, including views of the sunrise when Uluru glows iridescent orange – a phenomenon that on its own makes a visit worthwhile.

Opposite: *Uluru at sunset*
Above: *The western side of Uluru*

Above top: *Kata Tjuta*
Above bottom: *Uluru from the south*
Opposite above: *Uluru seen from Kata Tjuta*
Opposite middle: *Uluru in the setting sun*
Opposite below: *Uluru silhouetted at sunrise*

Connellan Airport is just a few kilometres from the small town of Yulara (Ayers Rock Resort). The only airline that flies there is Qantas and to get reasonable fares you should book well in advance. There are organized tours around the park, but hiring a car at the airport is hardly more expensive, even for a single traveller – though you should book in advance. A range of accommodation is available at Yulara, from a campsite to the new luxury Longitude 131° complex, and the town has a number of restaurants and shops. It is all run as a monopoly by one company so don't expect too much competition. The entrance fee gives access to the park for up to three days.

32

THE GHATS
Varanasi, India

Reputed to be the oldest living city in the world, having been continually inhabited for more than 4000 years, Varanasi (formerly Benares) is also one of the holiest places of Hinduism. It is so revered that the devout believe that just by dying there they can be freed from the endless cycle of rebirth.

The old Hindu name for Varanasi is Kashi – City of Light – and the quality of light here is truly spectacular. It is one of the few places in the world where this has inspired artists with its clarity and texture. It is best appreciated at sunrise as the faithful come down to the sacred River Ganges to bathe.

The narrow, tangled streets of the old town, Godaulia, all seem to lead to the Ganges. Flanking the river and leading down to the water are flights of stone steps called ghats. Many of these are hundreds of years old, some built by the maharajas whose palaces still tower over them.

The ghats teem with life: stalls sell everything from vegetables to religious icons, pandas (pilgrim priests) preach to the faithful, barbers shave the heads of pilgrims and mourners, sadhus (holy men) meditate and perform feats of yoga, boatmen ply for trade, dhobi-wallahs (washermen) beat laundry against the steps and small boys play enthusiastic games of cricket. Streams of pilgrims from all over India make their way through this activity to bathe in the river, believing that by doing so they can wash away their sins.

The best way to observe the bathing ritual is to take a rowing boat down the Ganges. This will

Opposite: *Rij Rama Palace on Darbhanga Ghat*

involve haggling with a boatman the day before you want to go, so ask at your hotel to get an idea of the correct price. Make sure you specify whether the price is per person or for the whole boat. (You might want to get this in writing to avoid the almost inevitable arguments later.)

Next morning, as you make your way to the river in the cold pre-dawn light, stumbling through the alleys of the old town and pushing past sacred cows that wander around freely, it will seem like a strange way to get to paradise. However, as soon as you are floating down the Ganges and the sun rises over the far bank, driving away the cold and bathing the ghats in soft golden light, you will forget the discomfort.

Hindus try to visit Varanasi at least once in their lifetime, and have to bathe at five different ghats to complete the pilgrimage. Hinduism is a joyful religion, and although bathing has great spiritual significance, the pilgrims laugh, splash, dive and push each other into the water.

It takes a few hours to travel the length of the river, fighting the current and stopping to watch the pilgrims and sadhus along the way. Get your boatman to drop you off at Manikarnika Ghat and walk back along the river to Dasasvamedha Ghat where most boat trips start.

Manikarnika is the cremation ghat. (Being cremated at Varanasi is yet another way to guarantee salvation, so many Hindu families go to great lengths to ensure their deceased loved ones undergo this ritual.) Bodies are brought from far away – sometimes on the roofs of buses – to be burnt here. Once at Varanasi, they are carried down to the ghat to chants of 'Ram Nam Satya Hai!' ('The name of god is truth!'). Firewood is haggled over, prayers are said, then the body is burnt and the ashes swept into the Ganges.

Opposite above: *Pilgrims bathing in the Ganges at Dasasvamedha Ghat*
Opposite below: *Pilgrims bathing in the Ganges*
Above: *Rowing down the Ganges*

Varanasi is easily reached by air from New Delhi or Kolkata (formerly Calcutta). There are also comfortable express trains, although you should try to take at least one old-style Indian train just for the experience. Accommodation boils down to a choice between quality and location. Hotels near the ghats are generally cheap but shoddy. Those of better quality, and therefore more expensive, tend to be in the new town. As with most things in India, the contrast between the two is often extreme. The better hotels organize day trips to Sarnath, the town about an hour away from Varanasi where the Lord Buddha gave his first sermon, and where there are a number of monuments and temples.

Above: *Sadhu running down the steps of Bhairavi Ghat*
Right: *A jewellery stall, Dasasvamedha Ghat Road*

The Ghats · Varanasi, India

33

HERON ISLAND
Great Barrier Reef, Australia

The Great Barrier Reef is a series of interlocking reefs and islands that stretch for over 2000 km in the waters off the coast of Queensland, Australia. It is the most extensive coral-reef system in the world, and the largest structure made completely from living organisms: tiny coral polyps.

Between 50 km and 300 km away from the shore, the reef comprises more than 2500 individual reefs (strips of rock or coral) and 600 islands. There are basically three types of island: continental islands (the peaks of sunken mountain ranges), sand islands and coral cays. Many of these islands have coral reefs nearby, or even mini-reefs fringing them, but Heron Island and the nearby Wilson Island are unique in that they are true coral cays that offer accommodation and actually form part of the reef. This means that you can simply swim from their beaches to dive or snorkel on the Great Barrier Reef itself.

The diving around Heron Island is reputed to be some of the best on the whole reef, attracting people from all over the world. The island has been leased out to the Heron Island Resort, which provides a range of accommodation, as well as diving and snorkelling excursions. Wilson Island is administered by Heron, and just 10 people are

Right: *Heron Island from the air*

allowed to stay on it at any one time. Those with a scientific interest in the reef can stay at the research centre on Heron Island, which is run by the University of Queensland.

From ground level, the barrier reef appears unexceptional. The sea might be a luxurious blue and the islands' sandy beaches creamy white, but little else is revealed unless you go up or down. From the air the true extent and colours of the Great Barrier Reef become apparent. Within waters of the purest turquoise, reef after reef seems to stretch away as far as you can see, and dotted around are tiny, white-fringed coral cays surrounded by their own reefs.

Heron Island · Great Barrier Reef, Australia

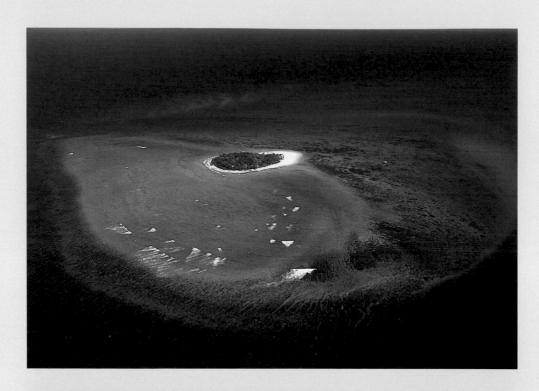

Heron Island · Great Barrier Reef, Australia

Diving or snorkelling on the reef is a truly magical experience, and no superlatives can do it justice. It's like experiencing a completely new world, where sight is the only sense you need and gravity seems irrelevant. Stick to shallow waters if you want to see the colours clearly, as deeper water filters out most of the red and green wavelengths, giving everything a deep blue tinge.

The coral is home to a wealth of life forms: multicoloured fish dart around at lightning speed, while green turtles and loggerheads take things at a more leisurely pace. At the top of Heron Island, in the aptly named Shark Bay, you will have a very good chance of being able to swim with the small and relatively friendly reef sharks.

If you don't fancy getting wet, the Heron Island Resort has a semi-submersible – basically a boat crossed with a submarine – where you can sit in the glass keel and view this underwater world in comfort.

You don't always have to go beneath the waves to see marine wildlife. Coming back from Wilson Island by boat, I came across a couple of migrating humpback whales. In the shallow waters of this part of the reef they were unable to dive deep, so I could hear them communicating with their haunting 'songs'. You are most likely to see migrating whales in September, while January and February are good times to see turtles laying eggs and the young eventually hatching.

Opposite above: Wilson Island fringed by reef
Opposite below: The reef near Heron Island
Above: Underwater coral

Heron Island · Great Barrier Reef, Australia

208

Quantas offer regular flights from Brisbane to Gladstone. From there, you can reach Heron Island by ferry or helicopter transfer – a good way to combine travel and seeing the reef from the air. There is one ferry daily, but it is available only to guests of the Heron Island Resort or to those staying at the research centre. Prices at the resort include all food and the quality is exceptional. Try to be there for the Saturday night seafood buffet. If you are not staying on the island the only way to visit it is by charter boat. As it is a marine park, diving and snorkelling among the reefs around the island are allowed.

Opposite left: *Coral on Wilson Island*
Opposite right: *Herons on the beach*
Above: *Beach at Heron Island*

Heron Island · Great Barrier Reef, Australia

34

LHASA

Tibet

It is not just the altitude that makes Lhasa a dizzying experience, although at nearly 4300 metres you get only 65 per cent of the oxygen you would get in each breath at sea level. That light-headed feeling comes in part from the deep spirituality of the place, and from the heady mix of juniper smoke and the ever-present smell of yak butter.

Expansion and modernization characterize the Chinese part of the city, but the old Tibetan quarter still has an ethereal, almost medieval atmosphere, especially in the network of small streets that surrounds the Jokhang Temple. The centre of Tibetan Buddhism, the Jokhang was completed in AD 647, although it has been continually restored and expanded ever since.

There are several distinct pilgrimage circuits around the Jokhang. The outer one, called the Lingkhor, runs around the entire city. The Barkhor, or middle route, is a circular road that runs round the outside of the temple.

Above: *The Potala Palace seen from the roof of the Jokhang*
Opposite: *Pilgrims walking the Nangkhor*

Above, top: *Pilgrims taking a break outside the Jokhang*

Left: *Khamba women on the Barkhor
with the Potala Palace behind*

Above: *Yak-butter lamps in the 1350-year-old Jokhang Temple*

Opposite: *Woman on the pilgrimage circuit around the Potala*

Lhasa · Tibet

Throughout the day and long into the night pilgrims process in a constant stream – always clockwise – around the Barkhor. Fearsome-looking Khambas (people from the eastern highlands), notable for the red threads braided into their hair, mingle with scarlet-robed monks and Golok nomads who wear huge sheepskin coats. Most spin prayer wheels as they walk, or mumble prayers which they keep count of on long strings of beads. Some stroll and chat, while others display penitence by repeatedly prostrating themselves along the route. Protected by leather aprons and with wooden paddles on their hands, they throw themselves across the paving flags, making a skittering sound that echoes around the Barkhor.

In the square in front of the Jokhang are two large braziers where pilgrims burn offerings of juniper: its pungent fragrance will for ever remind you of Lhasa. Also here is a small market, selling everything that the pilgrims might need for their devotions: yak butter, prayer flags, prayer wheels and, of course, fresh juniper.

Within the main porch of the temple are two giant prayer wheels, kept in constant motion by the streams of pilgrims. On the patio in front, pilgrims of all ages prostrate themselves time and again in a repetitive ritual, seemingly inured to the discomfort.

Inside the Jokhang, a double row of prayer wheels skirts the outside of the main prayer hall. This inner pilgrimage route is called the Nangkhor, and pilgrims walking around it attempt to spin each of the prayer wheels by hand to release their prayers up into the sky.

Inside the dark main hall of the Jokhang the air is heavy with the smell of yak-butter lamps, and the occasional low, rhythmic chanting of monks imparts a hallowed atmosphere that threatens to overwhelm the emotions. Pilgrims walk round the outside of the main hall – the centre being the exclusive preserve of monks, statues of former abbots and a giant golden Buddha image – past a number of small shrines and statues.

Towering above the whole city of Lhasa is the Potala Palace. The former home of the Dalai Lama, the spiritual leader of Tibetan Buddhism, it is now little more than a museum. I had feelings of both guilt and sadness as I walked through the private quarters, realizing that the Dalai Lama, rather than I, should have been there. Once situated on the outskirts of Lhasa, the Potala is now somewhat isolated in the middle of the modern part of the city. Around the base there is another pilgrimage route of prayer wheels which, like the Barkhor, is in constant use.

Above: *Entrance to the main prayer hall of the Jokhang*
Opposite: *Gilded roof of the Jokhang*

Tibet is a politically sensitive area, so the rules on visiting are subject to change without notice. You will need a special permit as well as a Chinese visa. The easiest way there is to take a tour from either Kathmandu or the city of Chengdu in China, although travellers from Nepal are often unable to change the duration of their permit once they arrive. Travellers from Chengdu can change the date of their return flight and effectively stay in Lhasa for the duration of their visa. Tours from both places can be arranged with other travellers in a couple of days. At the time of writing (2003) it was possible to travel independently from Chengdu only, however other routes are now available. Shigatse Travels, a travel agency based in Lhasa, can help and advise with arrangements. Most of the cheaper accommodation is in the Tibetan quarter. Many travellers feel that they should support Tibetan, rather than Chinese-run, businesses and are prepared to sacrifice comfort for atmosphere.

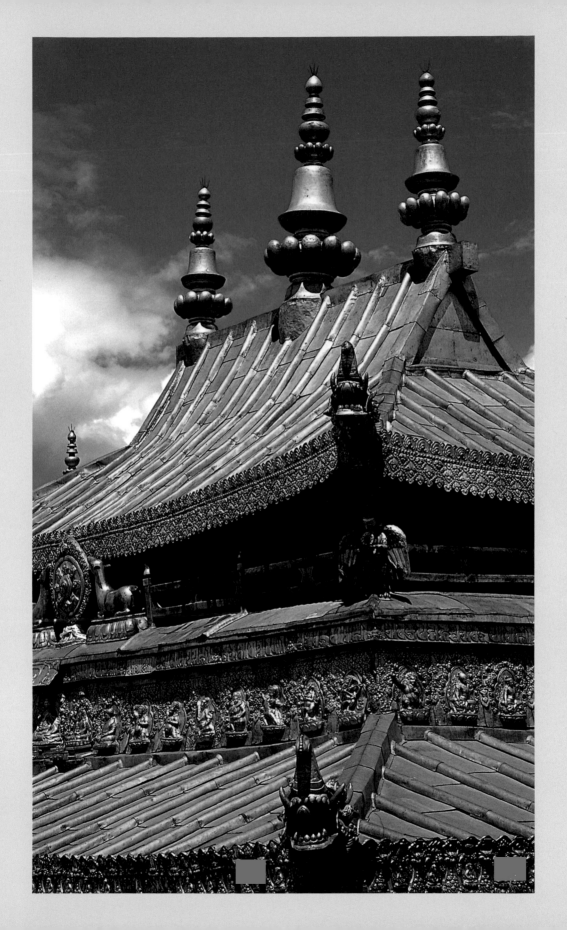

35

YANGSHUO
Guilin, China

The bustling tourist town of Guilin in Guangxi Province is famous across the world for its limestone peaks, which rise majestically from lush green rice paddies. However, the best scenery is further down the Li Jiang (Li River), at Yangshuo.

A number of official tourist boats ply this route, but they are primarily designed for the burgeoning domestic tourist market and drastically overcharge the foreigners they ferry down the river, in a long and decidedly unatmospheric convoy, then whisk them to Guilin by coach. A much better option is to take a bus from Guilin to Yangshuo and stay for a few days in this quiet town, hiring a bicycle and exploring the surrounding countryside at your leisure.

Areas with limestone peaks with eroded cavities and caves are described as 'karst'. Although other places have karst scenery –

including Vang Vieng in Laos and Viñales in Cuba – none has the complexity or the magnitude of that around Yangshuo. Spectacular limestone peaks stretch as far as the eye can see, and delight in such names as Lion Ascending Five Finger Hill or Grandpa Watching Apple.

It is best to go sightseeing in the early morning or late afternoon. Apart from avoiding the heat and humidity of the day, the light is better. (This type of landscape looks flat and hazy in the

Above: *Karst scenery just outside Yangshuo*
Opposite: *Views of peaks from Pantao Shan, Yangshuo*

midday light.) Sunrise and sunset are particularly evocative, even if the weather – exacerbated by the smog that seems to cover much of rapidly industrializing China – isn't perfect. The best position is at the top of one of the limestone peaks, and you should aim to climb at least a couple during your time here. The view from Yueliang Shan (Moon Hill) out to a sea of peaks bathed in early morning cloud is one of the most spectacular sights in the region, and well worth the 30-minute pre-dawn cycle ride and steep climb of similar duration to get there.

An almost equally stunning view of the sun slipping behind the peaks surrounding Yangshuo can be had from Pantao Shan, accessed via a steep and ragged path. The top is peppered with TV and radio masts, but gives almost a 360-degree panorama. Remember not to linger too long at the top or you will have to make the difficult journey back down in complete darkness.

About an hour by bus from Yangshuo is Xingping, from where you can take an unofficial boat trip to see some of the most impressive scenery on the river. You can sign up for this at any of the restaurants and guest houses in Yangshuo. Limestone mountains line the river on either side, offering a different view of the peaks and paddy fields around Yangshuo. Most trips also take in a 500-year-old fishing village once visited by former US president Bill Clinton.

Yangshuo · Guilin, China

On the outskirts of Xingping is probably the most well-known spot in the whole region: a bend in the river between limestone peaks, immortalized on the back of the current 20-yuan notes. The image and reality are identical – even down to an overhanging clump of bamboo. It is all remarkably unspoilt, especially given China's predilection for stringing up fairy lights and constructing eyesores that (with no trace of irony) they call 'place-for-viewing-the-unspoilt-landscape'.

Synonymous with the Guilin region – and appearing on most picture postcards – is cormorant fishing, which takes place on the river at night. Boat trips will take you out to see fishermen using trained cormorants to catch fish. (The training obviously leaves something to be desired, as the fishermen still feel the

Opposite: *Karst scenery at Xingping*
Above: *Craggy peak seen from Moon Hill, near Yangshuo*

Yangshuo · Guilin, China

219

Yangshuo · Guilin, China

need to tie string around the birds' throats to stop them swallowing the catch.) Alternatively, there are always a couple of cormorant fishermen hanging out during the day by the riverside at Yangshuo, who are willing to pose for pictures for a few yuan.

Left: *Bend in the river at Xingping, as it appears on 20-yuan notes*

Above: *Water buffalo at Xingping*

Yangshuo · Guilin, China

36

DUBROVNIK
Croatia

*Looking down on to the red-tiled roofs of the Old Town of Dubrovnik
as it nestles quietly alongside the cool waters of the Mediterranean,
it is hard to credit that its history is steeped in political intrigue, war
and destruction. But appearances are deceptive, and Dubrovnik
has a more violent and colourful past than most cities in Europe.*

For most of its long history Dubrovnik was an independent city state. It came under the protection of Venice in the 13th century, and Hungary some 150 years later. The city preserved its independence by careful diplomacy and payment of tributes. Under these conditions it grew into a wealthy democracy with a wide network of trading outposts. As

the importance of the city increased many civil construction projects, such as the city walls, were undertaken, and Dubrovnik proved attractive to writers and artists.

Below: *View of the city from the north*
Opposite: *Assumption of Mary Cathedral
seen from the city walls*

Although the sovereignty of Dubrovnik passed to the Ottoman Empire in the 16th century the city continued to flourish until it was all but destroyed by an earthquake in 1667. It was rebuilt in 1683, but the shifting trade allegiances and wars that rocked Europe during the 18th century weakened its power. The final death blow came in 1808, when Napoleon formally abolished Dubrovnik's tenuous independence, prompting a bombardment by British forces.

The city languished through subsequent wars and European politicking until it once again shot to prominence during the 1990s' Balkans War, following the break-up of Yugoslavia. During a siege which lasted seven months, before finally being lifted in May 1992, over 2000 shells slammed into the city.

Despite past violence and destruction, Dubrovnik is still a beautiful city. Indeed, the depredations of the siege have been repaired so successfully (with financial assistance from UNESCO) that visitors could be forgiven for thinking that war had never touched it.

The best way to get orientated in Dubrovnik is to walk around the towering and immensely thick 13th-century walls that surround the Old Town. At the highest point of the walls on the landward side of the city is the distinctive Minceta Tower, which has the best panoramic views of the city, Lokrum Island near the harbour mouth and the Mediterranean beyond. The battlements at the top of the tower give great views down into the narrow streets and courtyards. Church domes and spires reach above the expanses of red-tiled roofs, and at sunset golden light skims these roof tops and casts the skyline into relief against the surrounding landscape.

The main thoroughfare, the Stradun, divides the city into two halves and extends over 200 metres, from the Pile Gate in the west to the clock tower at the harbour entrance. Once a marsh that separated the Roman and Slavic halves of the city,

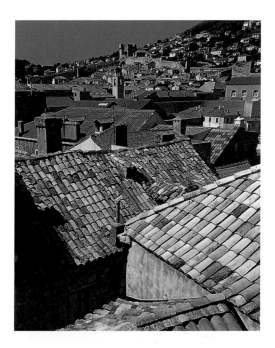

the Stradun is now paved with stones polished by years of pedestrian traffic, and lined with shops.

As you wander the narrow streets away from the Stradun, you get a sense of the tightly knit community. The houses in the Old Town are small and close together, with laundry strung between them, children play in the streets, and neighbours sit on front steps or lean from windows chatting and watching the world go by.

Positioned in the middle of some of the most beautiful coastline in Europe, Dubrovnik is the perfect place to while away a few days. Although it lacks the grandeur of Venice, and the power and influence it enjoyed in the 15th and 16th centuries has long since passed away, this small and modest city has a beguiling charm of its own.

Opposite above: *View from city walls with Lokrum Island in background*
Opposite below: *View of the city and the harbour*

Charter flights to Dubrovnik are available, but if you want the flexibility of a scheduled service your options are more limited. Alitalia fly there with a connection in one of three Italian cities. Alternatively, you can to fly to Belgrade and then take a domestic flight on Croatia Airlines. Dubrovnik offers a wide range of accommodation, but you should try and book during the summer months. Most of the better-quality accommodation is outside the city walls.

Above left: *The city walls dropping down into the Mediterranean*
Above right: *City walls and street below*
Opposite: *The Stradun (the main street of the city) seen from the city walls*

Dubrovnik · Croatia

37

EPHESUS

Turkey

The ruins at Ephesus are the best preserved of any Roman site in the Mediterranean. Although only 10 per cent of the city has been excavated, the wealth of surviving detail makes it easy to imagine the lives of the people who lived there: the latrines in the public baths are communal and packed close together; the brothel is across the street from the Library of Celsus; the agora, or market area, is vast, showing the importance of trade to the city; temples occur at frequent intervals; and a cemetery for gladiators has provided much information about their lives.

The ruins are spread along the slopes of two hills, with two level sites in between connected by the sloping Street of Curetes. The lower site, closest to the ancient harbour, has a vast amphitheatre that can seat 25,000 people. Concerts are still held here today.

Also on the lower site is the Library of Celsus, the single most impressive ruin at Ephesus, which is best seen at sunrise. All that remains is the front façade, with its entrances to the original building, and two huge storeys of pillars, statues and windows. Constructed using subtle techniques

Right: Columns on the way up to the Temple of Domitian
Opposite: View down the Street of the Curetes, from the Monument of Memmius (lower right) to the Library of Celsus

to manipulate perspective, the building, when viewed from ground level, appears much larger than it really is.

The Street of Curetes climbs upwards from the library, its wide pavement concealing sophisticated sewerage and water systems. On either side are columns and façades – the ruins of terraced housing, public baths with rows of latrines, a brothel, shops and temples.

Ephesus was founded by the Greeks, who arrived in the 10th or 11th century BC. Under their influence it became a mighty city and sea port, with a population of some 200,000 people. The Temple of Artemis (Diana), built during their time, was one of the Seven Wonders of the World. The present-day ruins, now about 5 km away from the coast, date from a city that was founded in the 3rd century BC by Lysimachus, one of Alexander

the Great's generals. The city came under Roman control in the 2nd century BC, and it later became an important centre of Christianity. (St Paul visited several times, and St John is said to be buried here.)

The Ephesus Museum in Selçuk has a great collection of artefacts and statues from Ephesus that will enhance your understanding of how the city must have looked, and what it might have been like to live there.

Above left: *Sunset over the amphitheatre*
Above top: *Temple of Hadrian*
Above: *Statue in the façade of the Library of Celsus*

The airport closest to Ephesus is at Izmir, which is 30 km away from the nearby town of Selçuk. The ruins are open from 8 a.m., which is just before summer sunrise strikes them directly. The gates close at 7 p.m. but you can generally wander around for at least another hour. The ruins are occasionally lit at night for special events, so it is worth finding out if your visit coincides with this impressive sight. Many people visit the site on day trips from beach locations such as Kusadasi, but if you want to really explore Ephesus you should stay in Selçuk, 3 km away. The best accommodation here is at the Hotel Kalehan.

Opposite: *Library of Celsus*
Above: *Library of Celsus*
Left: *The Agora near the Library of Celsus*

38

THE BUND
Shanghai, China

There are few cities in the world that have given rise to a verb, but it seems wholly appropriate that the frenetic city of Shanghai should have done so. 'To shanghai' originally meant to kidnap a drunken man and press him into work as a sailor, but it eventually came to mean compelling someone to do something by fraud or by force.

The verb fits the city that was once central to the commercial exploitation of China and much of Asia but had an underbelly steeped in vice, gambling, prostitution and opium. The British were granted the first trading concession in 1842 after the First Opium War, when the Chinese government was forced to relegalize the import of the drug. The commercial exploitation of China by Europe had begun. Great fortunes were made in trade and lost on the spin of a roulette wheel. Shanghai thrived on intrigue, catered to every kind of perversion and allowed criminal gangs to roam the streets. Not for nothing was the city known as the 'Whore of the Orient'.

Other countries – notably France – were later granted concessions, and soon a virtual European city existed. European Shanghai laid a thin veneer of respectability over the city with the creation of the Bund, an imposing stretch of buildings along the

Right: *Pudong, the Bund and the Huangpu River from the top of the Peace Hotel*

Huangpu River. Many were the head offices of great trading companies, insurance houses and banks. The most imposing, however, is the Customs House, one of the few buildings on the Bund that retains its original function. Another place worth checking out is the Peace Hotel, formerly the Cathay Hotel, once the most fashionable place in European Shanghai. The art deco interiors have recently been restored, and the hotel is probably the most atmospheric and historic place to stay in the city.

Although the vice and intrigue of Shanghai were suppressed by the Communists when they took charge of the city in 1949, they are now making a comeback.

The Bund · Shanghai, China

  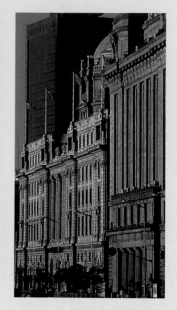

The Bund · Shanghai, China

In a uniquely Chinese demonstration of one-upmanship, the city authorities didn't demolish evidence of the colonial era — they merely dwarfed the buildings of the Bund, making them look insignificant. On one side of the Huangpu River, the Pudong New Area has been reclaimed from marshland, and since 1990 has become a massive area of tower blocks. The most spectacular are the Oriental Pearl TV Tower and the 88-storey Jinmao Tower, the top 35 floors of which house the Grand Hyatt Hotel. New skyscrapers, such as the Shanghai Tower, have since been built and are among the tallest buildings in the world.

As you look down from the top viewing-stage of the Oriental Pearl TV Tower or the Cloud Nine Bar at the top of the Hyatt Hotel, the sprawling towers of Shanghai seem to threaten the buildings of the Bund and push them into the river. Nonetheless, the Bund remains one of the most potent symbols of Shanghai, and from ground level it retains some of the gravitas and presence that it enjoyed in the past. It also remains the centre of Shanghai life. From the early morning, when it is thronged with kite flyers, old people practising t'ai chi and qi gong, and couples ballroom-dancing before work, to the daytime, when tourists from all over China flock to be photographed against the backdrop of the Bund and Pudong, through to the evening, when locals emerge to stroll in the cool breeze coming off the river, this stretch of waterfront is always packed and bursting with life.

Opposite above left: *Shopping by bicycle in the old streets of Shanghai*
Opposite above middle: *Outdoor laundry in the backstreets*
Opposite above right: *The Bund*
Opposite below: *View across to the Bund*
Above: *Looking down to the city from the top of the Oriental Pearl TV Tower*

The old streets of Shanghai can still be found in the Chinatown area of the city. Peculiar as it seems to have a Chinatown in a Chinese city, this area is a throwback to the days when Europeans ruled the roost and locals were restricted to certain parts of the city. A sign on the old British public gardens at the end of the Bund used to ban, among other things, dogs and Chinese.

Many of the old streets have been demolished to make room for the tower blocks of new Shanghai, and the rest are probably under threat in the headlong dash for progress. Among the surviving streets, some of the most atmospheric are between the old Yu Yuan (Jade Gardens) and the river. The gardens themselves are typically Chinese, created in the mid-16th century during the Ming dynasty. Shady pools, rock gardens and pagodas form a haven of peace in the noisy city, the atmosphere only slightly compromised by the Yu Yuan Bazaar, a sprawling 'old' themed shopping complex next door.

Life in the old streets of Shanghai seems to have remained unchanged for generations, and it is easy to imagine European sailors or traders staggering down alleys such as these in search of women or opium, never to be heard of again. The present, though, is less dramatic as daily life unfolds at a slow pace, punctuated by the constant chirruping of crickets kept in small bamboo cages for good luck.

Below: *Morning exercise on the Bund*
Opposite: *View of Pudong New Area from the Peace Hotel*

The Bund · Shanghai, China

Shanghai is one of the main international gateway cities of China and can be reached by air from most countries. Although there are many places to stay, the choice really comes down to the old – the atmospheric Peace Hotel right on the Bund – or the new, skyscraping Grand Hyatt Hotel. The city sprawls for miles, but most of the main sights are along the river – either along the Bund or in the reclaimed area of Pudong. There is a modern underground railway or you can catch a ferry across the river. A visit to see the famous Shanghai acrobats is a 'must'.

The Bund · Shanghai, China

39

SAMARKAND

Uzbekistan

The great city of Samarkand lies on the so-called Silk Road, the ancient trading route that led from China through the Middle East and into Europe. The city grew rich through trade, and constructed some of the finest buildings to be found in the Islamic world.

Its strategic position has led Samarkand to be conquered and sacked many times throughout its long and bloody history. The first settlement there was constructed in the 6th century BC and was first conquered by Alexander the Great some 200 years later. As trade routes built up over the next few hundred years, the city grew in power and wealth despite being captured by both the Turks and Hun tribes. Indeed, it continued to flourish, as recorded by the Buddhist monk and traveller Xuan Zang when he arrived there in AD 630.

At this time Samarkand followed the Zoroastrian religion of Persia, but the city fell to Islam when Qutaiba ibn Muslim invaded it in 712. This was the start of the first great period of Islamic development, which was curtailed at the beginning of the 13th century when the city was sacked by the Mongols of Genghis Khan, who slaughtered much of the population.

Above: *Dome of Tillya Kari Madrasa*
Opposite: *Dome and minaret of Bibi Khanum Mosque*

By the time another great traveller, Marco Polo, arrived at the end of the 13th century the city had been rebuilt, and he sang its praises. The Uzbek national hero, Tamerlane, chose it as the capital of the relatively small region of Transoxiana in 1370 and then proceeded to expand his empire until it reached as far as India and Syria. He was responsible for several great buildings, most notably the Bibi Khanum Mosque. His grandson, Uleg Beg, ruled the city until it fell to nomadic Uzbeks. Uleg Beg's great-grandson, Babur, retook the city in 1512 but was later driven out to India where he founded the Mogul Empire. This was the end of a golden era. Ravaged by earthquakes, looting and changing trade routes, Samarkand eventually succumbed to the Bolsheviks and became part of the Soviet Union in 1924.

The ancient centre of Samarkand is the Registan. This square, one of the finest in Asia, is surrounded on three sides by madrasas, or Islamic colleges. Uleg Beg constructed the square and the first madrasa in the 15th century. The fronts of the madrasas are towering façades that lead into ornate courtyards ringed with two storeys of small cells where the religious students lived and studied.

Ironically, for all their anti-religious sentiment and public denigration of Islam, it was the Soviets who restored much of the Registan, straightening precarious minarets and reconstructing the characteristic turquoise-tiled domes. These still

Opposite: *Cell where Islamic students would study*
Below left: *Detail of Bibi Khanum Mosque*
Below right: *Shir Dor Madrasa*

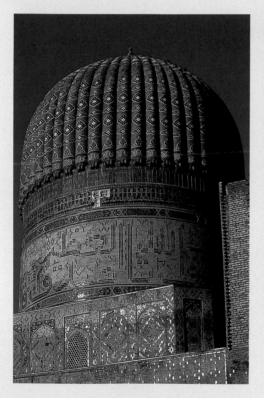

shine with an iridescence that perhaps suggests the cool water that is often lacking in this dry land.

Islam forbids the representation of living things, so each of the madrasas is covered with ornate patterns (none symmetrical, as this too is forbidden), intricate Kufic quotations from the Koran and inscriptions extolling the magnificence of the buildings. Bizarrely, though, the Shir Dor Madrasa on the eastern side of the square has two representations of lions in front of suns with shining human faces. This apparent heresy is attributed in part to the ego of the governor who built the madrasa and also to the continued influence of the Persian Zoroastrians who revered the power of the sun.

The Uleg Beg and Shir Dor madrasas are flanked by minarets, used more for decoration than for calling the faithful to prayer as the buildings were primarily colleges rather than mosques. In Tamerlane's day, however, they were also used for public executions: a favourite way of dealing with criminals was to throw them from the top in a sack.

For a couple of dollars, one of the uniformed guards might let you climb the crumbling steps to the top of the north minaret at Ulug Beg Madrasa for one of the most impressive views across the city to the Bibi Khanum Mosque. Tamerlane constructed this vast mosque from the finest materials after sacking the city of Delhi in 1398.

In the adjacent bazaar life and trade continue much as they did when the Silk Road brought spices, gold and fabrics to be traded here. You can still buy the round hats worn by many of Uzbekistan's Muslims, decorated flat breads and exotic spices that hark back to the days when peppercorns and saffron were more valuable than gold.

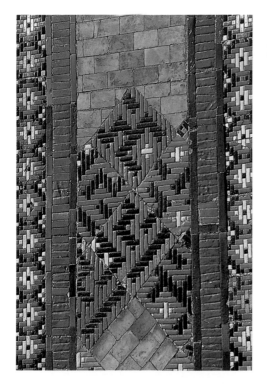

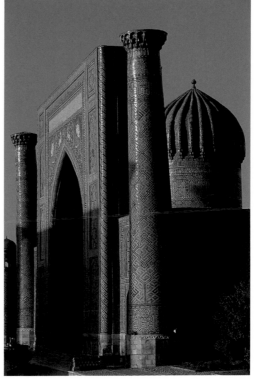

Samarkand is easily reached by bus or air from the capital Tashkent. Several airlines fly to Tashkent. Uzbekistan Air has a remarkably modern fleet and a fairly good worldwide network. Buying a domestic ticket overseas can be difficult, so you will probably find it easier to attach it to your international flight. Hotel accommodation is plentiful in Samarkand, including the four-star Hotel Presidential Palace.

Opposite: *Shir Dor Madrasa*
Above left: *Shir Dor Madrasa*
Above right: *Detail of Registan Square*
Above: *Shir Dor Madrasa*

Samarkand · Uzbekistan

40

KILLARY HARBOUR
Connemara, Ireland

Connemara is an area that for many people best encapsulates what is great and beautiful about Ireland and its desolate west coast. The jagged coastline has many bays and inlets, none of which is more striking than Killary Harbour – a dramatic meeting of mountains and sea on the border between County Galway and County Mayo.

Separating the Mweelrea and Sheefry mountains on the north shore from the Maumturk Mountains and the Twelve Bens on the south shore, the harbour is actually Ireland's only fjord. It was formed during the last ice age, when characteristic U-shaped valleys were carved between the mountains by glaciers, which then melted causing the sea to rise and flood the harbour.

About 1.5 km north of the harbour, in Mayo, is the Delphi Lodge and further up the valley is the beautiful and rugged Lough Doo. In 1849 potato-famine victims made the arduous trek from north Mayo through Lough Doo Pass to Delphi Lodge, and many people died along the way.

South of the harbour, a few kilometres beyond Lough Fee, is Kylemore Abbey, dramatically located at the base of Duchruach Mountain on the shore of Lough Pollacappul and home to Benedictine nuns. The coast, beaches and roads around Renvyle on the south side of the

Right: Ballynakill Harbour, County Galway

harbour's mouth have the best views of the harbour and its mountains, and of the island of Inishbofin.

The Western Way hiking trail passes through Connemara and all the mountain ranges around the harbour. The stretch of trail above the harbour west of Leenane gives a great view of the sun setting at the mouth of the harbour, and of the islands within it.

The village of Leenane, at the very end of the harbour, is often called the 'Gateway to Connemara'. It boasts great views across the harbour, and two lively pubs which, for this part of Ireland, make it almost a metropolis. Whether you

Killary Harbour · Connemara, Ireland

duck inside to avoid one of the regular showers of rain or linger all night to celebrate a perfect sunset, you will find enough of the legendary Irish craic (good times) to keep you entertained.

The weather in this part of the world can be dramatic and very variable, thanks to the mountains and the Atlantic Ocean creating localized conditions that can change from minute to minute. The peak of Mweelrea Mountain, the highest in Connemara, is almost always hidden by cloud, even on the clearest days, and storms can suddenly sweep through the area. But when the weather is good in Connemara, there is no more beautiful place to be.

The three airports nearest to Killary Harbour are at Galway, Shannon and Dublin. Driving to Leenane from these airports takes 1 1/2 hours, 3 hours and 5–6 hours, respectively. The nearest large town is Clifden, where there is a wide choice of accommodation. There are also hotels and campsites throughout the area. The weather can be rough but it changes very quickly – if you drive from place to place, the good weather will find you. High summer is the best, though most crowded, time but conditions are very similar between May and September.

Opposite above: *Sunset at Renvyle, County Galway*
Opposite below: *Lough Doo*
Above top: *Grass on beach dunes at Doovilra, County Mayo*
Overleaf: *View of the mouth of Killary Harbour from near Tully Cross, County Galway, with Mweelrea in background*

Killary Harbour · Connemara, Ireland

1. **Angkor Wat** · Cambodia
2. **St Petersburg** · Russia
3. **Havana** · Cuba
4. **Wat Phra Kaeo** · Bangkok, Thailand
5. **Grand Canyon** · Arizona, USA
6. **Taj Mahal** · Agra, India
7. **Eilean Donan Castle** · Scotland
8. **The Alhambra** · Granada, Spain
9. **Aitutaki** · Cook Islands
10. **Pyramid of Kukulcán** · Mexico

11. **Venice** · Italy
12. **Dead Vlei** · Namibia
13. **Iguassu Falls** · Brazil and Argentina
14. **Petra** · Jordan
15. **College Fjord** · Alaska, USA
16. **Karnak Temple** · Luxor, Egypt
17. **Rio de Janeiro** · Brazil
18. **Taman Negara Rainforest** · Malaysia
19. **Jaisalmer Fort** · India
20. **Galapagos Islands** · Ecuador

21. Manhattan Island · New York, USA

22. Lake Titicaca · Bolivia and Peru

23. Monet's Garden · Giverny, France

24. Ngorogoro Crater · Tanzania

25. Santorini · Greece

26. The Amphitheatre · Drakensberg, South Africa

27. Zanzibar · Tanzania

28. Makalu · Himalayas, Nepal

29. Lalibela · Ethiopia

30. Machu Picchu · Peru

31. Uluru · Australia

32. The Ghats · Varanasi, India

33. Heron Island · The Great Barrier Reef, Australia

34. Lhasa · Tibet

35. Yangshuo · Guilin, China

36. Dubrovnik · Croatia

37. Ephesus · Turkey

38. The Bund · Shanghai, China

39. Samarkand · Uzbekistan

40. Killary Harbour · Ireland

USEFUL WEB ADDRESSES

Cambodia

Bangkok Airways
www.bangkokair.com

Amansara Resort
www.aman.com

Ministry of Tourism
www.tourismcambodia.org/mot

St Petersburg, Russia

Intourist
www.intourist.com

Cuba

Ministry of Tourism
www.cubatravel.cu

Thailand

Tourism Authority of Thailand
www.tourismthailand.org

USA

Grand Canyon
El Tovar Lodge
www.grandcanyonlodges.com

The National Parks Department
www.nps.gov/grca

New York
www.iloveny.com

Alaska
www.travelalaska.com

India

Ministry of Tourism
www.tourism.gov.in

Scotland

Scottish Tourist Board
www.visitscotland.com

Spain

Spanish Tourist Board
www.tourspain.es

Paradores of Spain
www.parador.es

Cook Islands

Air Rarotonga
www.airaro.com

Aitutaki Pacific Resort
www.pacificresort.com

Cook Islands Tourism
www.cookislands.travel

Mexico

Mayaland Hotel
www.mayaland.com

Mexican Tourist Board
www.visitmexico.com

Venice

Tourist Board of Venice
www.turismovenezia.it

Namibia

Wilderness Safaris Namibia
www.wilderness-safaris.com

Namibia Tourism
www.namibiatourism.com.na

Jordan

Royal Jordanian Airways
www.rj.com

Jordan Tourism Board
www.visitjordan.com

Mövenpick
www.moevenpick-hotels.com

Egypt

Egyptian State Tourist Office
www.touregypt.net

Egyptair
www.egyptair.com

Brazil

Brazil Tourist Board
www.embratur.gov.br

Macuco Safari
www.macucosafari.com.br

Helisight, Rio de Janeiro
www.helisight.com.br

Malaysia

Taman Negara Resort
www.mutiaratamannegara.com

Tourism Malaysia
www.tourism.gov.my

Galapagos

Metropolitan Touring
www.metropolitan-touring.com

Ministry of Tourism
www.vivecuador.com

Lake Titicaca and Machu Picchu

Peru Tourist Board
www.peru.travel

Giverny, France

Information website
www.giverny.org

Tanzania

Sopa Lodge, Ngorongoro Crater
www.sopalodges.com

Abercrombie & Kent Travel
www.abercrombiekent.com

Air Excel
www.airexcelonline.com/en

Tanzania Tourist Board
www.tanzaniatourism.com.tz

Santorini, Greece

Santorini Hotels
online booking service
www.santorini-hotels.net

Greek national
Tourism Organization
www.gnto.gr

Republic of South Africa

Ezemvelo KZN Wildlife
www.kznwildlife.com

Nepal

Nepal Tourism Board
www.welcomenepal.com

Ethiopia

Ethiopian Airlines
www.ethiopianairlines.com

Ethiopian Tourism Commission
www.ethiopia.travel

Australia

Qantas
www.qantas.com.au

Ayers Rock Resort
www.ayersrockresort.com.au

Heron Island Resort
www.heronislandresort.com.au

Australian Tourist Commission
www.australia.com

Tibet

Tibet Government in Exile
www.tibet.net

China Tourism
www.chinatour.net

China

Peace Hotel, Shanghai
www.fairmont.com

China Tourism
www.chinatour.net

Dubrovnik, Croatia

Croatian National Tourist Office
www.croatia.hr

Hotel Kompas, Dubrovnik
www.adriaticluxuryhotels.com

Ephesus, Turkey

Hotel Kalehan, Selçuk
www.kalehan.com

Republic of Turkey, Ministry of
Culture and Tourism
www.turizm.gov.tr

Samarkand, Uzbekistan

Cox and Kings Travel
www.coxandkings.co.uk

Tourism Uzbekistan
www.tourism.uz

Ireland

Renvyle House Hotel,
County Galway
www.renvyle.com

Tourism Ireland
www.tourismireland.com

ACKNOWLEDGEMENTS

The following organizations have contributed material support and assistance with the travel and photographic arrangements. We thank them for their vision and their generosity. Without them this project would not have been possible.

Photography

Classic Photographic, London. **India:** Indian Trends, Delhi; Naryan Niwas Palace. **Cook Islands:** Air Rarotonga; Aitutaki Pacific Resort; Cook Islands Tourism. **Mexico:** Mayaland Hotel. **Venice:** The Europa and Regina Hotel. **Namibia:** Wilderness Safaris Namibia. **Brazil:** Brazil Tourist Board; Las Cataratas Hotel; Macuco Safari; Helisul Helicopter Tours, Foz do Iguaçu; Helisight, Rio de Janeiro. **Jordan:** Royal Jordanian; Jordan Tourism Board. **Malaysia:** Taman Negara Resort. **Galapagos:** Metropolitan Touring. **Lake Titicaca and Machu Picchu:** South American Experience, London; Orient Express. **Tanzania:** Sopa Lodge, Ngorongoro Crater; Abercrombie & Kent Travel; Air Excel; Hotel Arusha. **Republic of South Africa:** Ezemvelo KZN Wildlife. **Ethiopia:** Ethiopian Airlines. **Australia:** Qantas; Ayers Rock Resort; Heron Island Resort; Northern Territory Tourist Commission. **China:** Peace Hotel, Shanghai. **Dubrovnik:** Croatian National Tourist Office; Hotel Kompas, Dubrovnik. **Ephesus:** Hotel Kalehan; Republic of Turkey, Ministry of Culture and Tourism. **Ireland:** Renvyle House Hotel; Tourism Ireland.

And finally, special thanks to Marc Schlossman, who photographed the following locations for this book: St Petersburg, Eilean Donan Castle, Dead Vlei, College Fjord, the Galapagos Islands, Manhattan Island, Lake Titicaca, Giverny, Drakensberg, Makalu, Machu Picchu, Dubrovnik, Ephesus and Killary Harbour.

10 9 8 7 6 5 4 3 2 1

BBC Books, an imprint of Ebury Publishing
20 Vauxhall Bridge Road
London SW1V 2SA

BBC Books is part of the Penguin Random House group of companies whose addresses can be found at global.penguinrandomhouse.com

Penguin
Random House
UK

Text copyright © Steve Davey 2004, 2019
Photographs copyright © Steve Davey and Marc Schlossman
Photograph of orcas on page 99
© Jeff Pantukhoff/Seapics.com

The author has asserted his right to be identified as the author of this Work in accourdance with the Copyright, Designs and Patents Act 1988.

First published by BBC Books in 2004
This edition published by BBC Books in 2019

www.penguin.co.uk

A CIP catalogue record for this book is available from the British Library

ISBN 9781785944161

Commissioning editor: Nicky Ross
Project editor: Christopher Tinker
Copy-editor: Trish Burgess
Art director: Linda Blakemore
Designer: James Pople

Printed and bound in China by C&C Offset Printing Co., Ltd

Penguin Random House is committed to a sustainable future for our business, our readers and our planet. This book is made from Forest Stewardship Council® certified paper.

MIX
Paper from responsible sources
FSC® C018179